Praise for *How to End Christian Nationalism*

"Amanda Tyler is a powerful sister who has led Christians in a movement to counter the religious nationalists who do so much evil in God's name. May this resource help others learn from her experience and wisdom."

—**William J. Barber II**, co-chair of Poor People's Campaign, professor and founding director of the Center for Public Theology & Public Policy at Yale Divinity School, and author of *White Poverty* and other books

"Amanda Tyler's book is an indispensable tool in renewing civic engagement and democracy in America in these polarizing times. With the rise of theocratic and authoritarian organizations, *How to End Christian Nationalism* is a foundational text for anyone who cares not only about America's past but about its future."

—**Anthea Butler**, author of *White Evangelical Racism* and Geraldine R. Segal Professor in American Social Thought and chair of religious studies at the University of Pennsylvania

"Clear, concise, and compelling, *How to End Christian Nationalism* is the perfect book for anyone confused about

Christian nationalism and wondering what they can do about it. All American Christians who love their country would do well to read this book and take its lessons to heart."

—**Kristin Kobes Du Mez**, author of *Jesus and John Wayne: How White Evangelicals Corrupted a Faith and Fractured a Nation*

"*How to End Christian Nationalism* is essential reading for those of us who seek to follow Jesus in the Way. Amanda Tyler is clear, focused, learned, and passionate in defining Christian nationalism as the threat it is—to democracy and to the faith of Jesus—and providing a map to end the grip it has on too much of our nation. White Christians are a key audience here, but Christians of every ethnicity can learn from this important text."

—**Jacqui Lewis**, senior minister and public theologian at Middle Collegiate Church

"With the precision of an attorney and the practicality of an organizer and advocate, Amanda Tyler helps us see what we can do to defeat the biggest threat to American democracy today: white Christian nationalism. This timely and insightful book does more than just sound the alarm; it passionately lays out a call to action."

—**Robert P. Jones**, *New York Times* bestselling author of *The Hidden Roots of White Supremacy* and other books

"*How to End Christian Nationalism* chillingly describes the insidious forces pushing the false narratives that fueled the

January 6 attack on the US Capitol, the Unite the Right rally in Charlottesville, Virginia, and many of the mass shootings that have plagued the country in recent years. Amanda Tyler seamlessly weaves history with modern statistics and polling data to illustrate how Christian nationalism perverts Scripture into a tool to build power and justify political violence. The book offers a sound prescription for challenging the extremist ideology that has infected America's politics in a particularly critical time."

—**Mary B. McCord**, executive director of the Institute for Constitutional Advocacy and Protection, visiting professor of law at Georgetown University Law Center, and former Acting Assistant Attorney General for National Security at the US Department of Justice

"What can we do to fight Christian nationalism? What is the responsibility of those Christians who share a faith tradition but certainly not theological, political, or ethical affinities with their Christian nationalist siblings? Using stories from her own life and insight gained from decades of political activism for a gospel based on justice and equality, Tyler offers a plea to all Christians to do the work of joining diverse coalitions of Americans who will stand together against Christian nationalism. There is no one more equipped to offer strategies for combating one of the gravest threats to our democracy. Tyler is a prophetic witness—someone who has given testimony in churches and in front of Congress about the ways Christian nationalism is destroying both our public square and the foundations of American Christianity. In a time when Christian nationalism is ascendant, hope springs from organizing. *How to End Christian Nationalism* provides both the call to action and the strategy for victory."

—**Bradley Onishi**, author of *Preparing for War*, founder of Axis Mundi Media, and president of the Institute for Religion, Media, and Civic Engagement

"The United States is the most religiously diverse nation in human history. To achieve our potential as a country, we must welcome the contributions of people of all faiths and none, and strengthen the bonds between them. To do that, we must defeat the scourge of Christian nationalism. This book will show you how."

—**Eboo Patel**, founder and president of Interfaith America and author of *We Need to Build: Field Notes for Diverse Democracy*

"In her soulful, unflinching, and powerful new book, Amanda Tyler gives all Americans—but especially serious Christians like herself—the means of constitutional, theological, political, and psychological self-defense against the toxic ideology of white Christian nationalism. Anyone who has wondered about the relationship between this surging fanaticism and what happened on January 6 should look no further. This book is a labor of love for Tyler's country and her faith, and it is a gift to America in dangerous times."

—**Jamie Raskin**, attorney, law professor, and US Representative for Maryland's 8th Congressional District

"Amanda Tyler is the right person at the right time with the right book to clearly and compellingly explain the urgent and growing threat of Christian nationalism. For white Christians like myself, Tyler's book offers an altar call to join together to end Christian nationalism as an act of devotion to our faith, and patriotic duty to our country."

—**Paul Brandeis Raushenbush**, president and CEO of Interfaith Alliance

"In *How to End Christian Nationalism*, Amanda Tyler offers a deeply compelling call to action and a practical and timely guide for how we can reclaim the integrity of our faith from the heresy of Christian nationalism and, in the process, protect and strengthen a pluralistic and more inclusive democracy."

—**Adam Russell Taylor**, president of Sojourners and author of *A More Perfect Union*

"If you have ever asked the question 'What do we do about white Christian nationalism?' then you simply must get your copy of *How to End Christian Nationalism*. With the precision of a constitutional lawyer and the heart of a public servant, Amanda Tyler offers practical steps to protect religious freedom for all. White Christian nationalism is the greatest threat to democracy and the witness of the church in the United States today. But we are not powerless, and *How to End Christian Nationalism* is a potent tool for taking action."

—**Jemar Tisby**, *New York Times* bestselling author of *The Color of Compromise, How to Fight Racism*, and *The Spirit of Justice*, and professor of history at Simmons College of Kentucky

"As concern is rising over the ascendancy of authoritarianism, attacks on our democracy, religious extremism, and blurred lines between church and state, *How to End Christian Nationalism* arrives right on time. Lawyer, advocate, organizer, mother, and Christian faith leader Amanda Tyler offers a clear and compelling picture of the influence of white Christian nationalism in US society. But rather than just cursing the darkness, Tyler, the lead organizer of Christians Against Christian Nationalism, shines a light on the path to bring 'good news' of love, truth, hope, and justice in its place and invites all—especially white Christians—to join her."

—**Liz Theoharis**, director of Kairos Center for Religions, Rights, and Social Justice; co-chair of Poor People's Campaign; and editor of *We Cry Justice*

"The answer to bad religion is not no religion but good faith. I am so grateful that Amanda Tyler has made it her life calling to challenge the false religion of Christian nationalism, embedded in white supremacy, with true faith in Jesus Christ. Strong on both analysis and strategy, she keeps quoting the Bible (as good Baptists do!) to dismantle this idolatry that puts power over love. She shows how the separation of church and state does not require the segregation of moral and religious values from public life, but calls for faithful, just, and humble prophetic witness."

—**Jim Wallis**, inaugural Archbishop Desmond Tutu Chair in Faith and Justice at Georgetown University and author of *The False White Gospel* and other books

How to End Christian Nationalism

How to End Christian Nationalism

Amanda Tyler

BROADLEAF BOOKS
MINNEAPOLIS

29 28 27 26 25 24   1 2 3 4 5 6 7 8 9

Library of Congress Control Number: 2024934607 (print)

Cover design: Studio Gearbox

Print ISBN: 978-1-5064-9828-7
eBook ISBN: 978-1-5064-9829-4

Contents

Introduction

He has told you, O mortal, what is good, and what does the Lord require of you but to do justice and to love kindness and to walk humbly with your God?

—Micah 6:8 (NRSVUE)

"When did you become radicalized about Christian nationalism?"

The question from the journalist jarred me. I had never thought of myself as a radical about anything. I'm a mild-mannered person, and friends have long remarked on my ability to remain outwardly calm and collected in stressful situations. As an attorney, I've spent my career steeped in rational inquiry, measured analysis, and logical argument. I'm a lifelong Baptist, and I lead a religious advocacy group, so I spend a lot of time preaching, participating in Bible studies, serving on church committees, and going to potlucks.

I'm also a mother, so I have volunteered for the PTA, packed countless lunches, and read many bedtime stories. I wasn't sure what was so radical about days spent reading Supreme Court opinions, writing sermons, and making dinner for my family.

I also associate the term *radicalized* with extremist violence, something that must be roundly condemned no matter its source. We see radicalization all around us in the nation and the world, and I had never thought of the term as having anything to do with me. How did working to maintain the separation of church and state and to protect faith freedom for all people become *radical*?

But the reporter's question was telling. She was correct that I had taken up this cause—to dismantle Christian nationalism, particularly in white Christian communities—as my life's calling. She was also correct that a white Christian working to uproot instead of perpetuate Christian nationalism was still something of a rarity. A Christian countering Christian nationalism was sufficiently different from what she expected that it appeared radical, even extreme. What a sad commentary on our times.

I hope to make the idea of a Christian working to end Christian nationalism the norm rather than the exception, and I am inviting you to help me. In my years of studying and then speaking about Christian nationalism in churches, community centers, campuses, and countless Zoom rooms, I have learned that a large and diverse community of people is eager to challenge the political ideology of Christian nationalism.

But the problem can seem too big and amorphous to know where to start. This book lays out a step-by-step process for exploring the problem of Christian nationalism and taking action to defend religious freedom for all.

We will not end Christian nationalism if Christians do not actively work to dismantle it: to rid it from ourselves, our congregations, and our larger communities. For Christians who are committed to this cause, basing our activism in our faith provides the motivation and the sustenance to persevere in this hard work. And make no mistake: this will not be an easy road. Christian nationalism is deeply entrenched in US society. Because generations have let Christian nationalism fester, the ideology has grown deep roots, creating an underground system that makes it that much harder to extricate. Nor can this outcome—ending Christian nationalism—be accomplished in my lifetime or yours. We must accept that a problem that has gone unaddressed for centuries will take several generations to resolve. This book offers a starting place for each person willing to contribute to this multigenerational project. It does not, however, make false promises about how smoothly or quickly this work will go.

I hope this book will be helpful to you no matter who you are. I expect it will be particularly useful for my fellow Christians—particularly white Christians—who are feeling compelled to respond to Christian nationalism. I have included references to scripture throughout these pages so that we can continually ground ourselves in the biblical tradition. Billions of people across two millennia have found the Christian scriptures formative, and we can find inspiration and support for our work for faith freedom for all in the words of sacred text.

In various points in this book, we will explore how deeply interconnected racism is with Christian nationalism. White Christians need to learn the history, question assumptions, and be willing to shift our own narratives about what it means to be Christian and what it means to be American. We also need to raise our self-awareness—particularly our awareness about the power we hold because of our whiteness—to avoid the very real danger of perpetuating white Christian nationalism in our efforts to dismantle it.

Though my primary audience is white Christians who want to engage in this long-haul work of ending Christian nationalism, I hope this book will also be a helpful resource to people of color, people from other religious traditions, and people who are nonreligious who are part of or want to join the large movement to end Christian nationalism.

The scripture that begins this introduction is one around which I have oriented my life. These words from Micah 6:8 were read as I walked across the stage at my law school graduation. They were spoken at my wedding, and they inspired my Jewish husband and me to give our son the name Micah at his blessing ceremony. The commandment— to do justice, love kindness, and walk humbly with God—is elegantly simple yet endlessly challenging. Doing justice in a world rife with injustice and inequality is a never-ending task. Loving kindness recalls the centrality of human relationship to life and of Jesus's commandment to show love for God by showing love for our neighbors. Walking humbly both acknowledges our humanity and imperfection and reminds us that we are never alone in this work. God is with us.

I consider this book to be an act of doing justice, loving kindness, and walking humbly. I undertake this project with humility, knowing that a vast community of organizers, advocates, activists, scholars, journalists, faith leaders, lawyers, and others is engaged in this work. My hope is that my story, and the stories and wisdom of others I share here, will inspire an even larger group of people to join this cause.

MY STORY

My journey to end Christian nationalism began nearly forty years ago, when I made my profession of faith in the baptismal waters at Riverbend Baptist Church in Austin, Texas. As a seven-year-old, confidently making my decision to follow Jesus, I had already experienced one of life's hardest moments: the death of a close loved one. My younger sister was born with a serious heart defect, and she died when she was just twenty months old. I was three and a half when Katy was born and five years old when she died. My faith provided me great comfort during those difficult days of grief and confusion. I also experienced the best of a church community as our pastor, ministerial staff, deacons, and friends from church gathered around my family.

Around the same time as my baptism, I also set my sights on a life in law and politics. Now that I have a child around the same age as I was then, I can see how precocious and unusual my professional choice was. No one in my family was a lawyer or public servant. But when our state senator paid a visit to my second-grade class for Career Day, I was mesmerized. I remember asking him how to become a senator, and he said to go to law school.

My life has proceeded along these two tracks of religion and government. Church has always been a large part of my life, and while I am not ordained, I have been an active lay member of several Baptist churches and one Episcopal church. During my childhood, you would have found me in my Baptist church two or three times a week—for Sunday school and worship on Sunday mornings, Wednesday night fellowship meal and kids' activities, and as I grew older, Sunday night youth group. I attended and then volunteered for Vacation Bible School every summer. I went on mission trips and chaperoned youth camp during my college years. My mom was an adult Sunday school teacher, and some of our closest family friends were members of her class. My dad sang in the church choir.

My interest in both religion and politics led me to undergraduate study at Georgetown University, the country's oldest Catholic and Jesuit university. At Georgetown, I lived and studied with people from different faith traditions, and I learned that faith and questioning not only are compatible, they are inseparable. I regularly attended Catholic mass and was an active member of various Protestant student groups as well.

As a first-year student at Georgetown, I encountered the work of the Baptist Joint Committee for Religious Liberty (BJC), the organization that I now lead. BJC has been a faith-based voice for religious freedom for all and the separation of church and state since 1936. I remember an October afternoon in 1996 when a lay leader from the church I'd attended as a teenager visited Washington, DC, and took me to meet the staff of BJC.

I vividly recall a day toward the end of the fall semester of my sophomore year when the general counsel, Brent Walker, called me to say there was an opening for an internship at BJC and asked if I could spare some time to help for a few months. As an intern, I learned about how Baptists had long advocated for religious freedom for all, and I gained a more in-depth appreciation for constitutional law. That internship developed into a staff position my senior year. Then, on a sweltering day in August 2001, I packed up a U-Haul truck and drove cross-country with my dad back to Austin to start school at the University of Texas School of Law. During law school, I continued my interest in constitutional law and politics and reconnected with my church home at Highland Park Baptist Church.

After law school, I moved to Dallas to work for a civil litigation firm that also was politically active, allowing me to continue my interest in both law and government. I also found a small faith community called City Church that nurtured and developed my spirituality as a young adult. It was during my time in Dallas that I met my husband. Robert is from a different faith tradition than I am—Reform Judaism. For the first time, I was in a close relationship with someone who practiced a different religion from me. Loving people—Robert, his family, and his friends—who are not Christians made religious freedom become even more real and important to me.

In 2009, I joined the staff of US Representative Lloyd Doggett (D-Texas) as the district director in Austin. It was the beginning of the Obama administration, and the new president had taken on as his top priority the passage of major health care reform legislation. By that summer, politically conservative action groups were mobilizing people to oppose passage of the law by any means necessary.

One hot Saturday morning in August, I arrived early at a grocery store to set up for the congressman's "neighborhood office hours." An angry mob soon descended on the parking lot, shouting down the event and waving hateful signs, including one with Rep. Doggett's name on a tombstone and another where his eyes had been altered to appear demonic. At future events, I noticed that many of the same activists would show up brandishing assault-style rifles. Looking back, I see those intimidation tactics as a foreshadowing of what was to come, years later, when a violent mob, fueled by similar vitriol and Christian nationalist ideologies, would storm the US Capitol on January 6, 2021.

My eight years working with Rep. Doggett—first in Texas and later as his counsel for the Ways and Means Committee in Washington—taught me an enormous amount about public service and the legislative process. Most importantly, I got a front-row view of how difficult it is for our elected representatives to reflect the views of their diverse constituencies in making just laws for our pluralistic society, particularly with the pressure of moneyed interests bombarding Congress.

But in 2016, around the time of my son's first birthday, I sensed a new call, this time to an office on just the other side of Capitol Hill. It was physically close but represented a move out of government and into nonprofit advocacy: leading BJC. Advocating for the separation of church and state for more than eight decades now, BJC works from the historic Baptist tradition of "soul freedom": the theological idea that every person must have the freedom to respond to God and that no governmental authority should interfere with that relationship. Our advocacy is often for those whose beliefs differ from our own because Christians hold and have always held power in the United States.

The BJC Board of Directors affirmed my call six weeks before the 2016 presidential election. At the time, conventional wisdom was that the country would elect the first female president, Hillary Clinton. Her views on protecting religious freedom were largely in line with BJC's advocacy. In short, the biggest challenges at the time seemed to be weakening protections of religious liberty at the US Supreme Court. Clinton was someone who would appoint future justices who would likely share her views of religious freedom.

But then came November 8, 2016, the night Donald J. Trump was elected president. I remember the dread I felt that night because I knew the campaign promises Trump had made. He proposed "a total and complete shutdown of Muslims entering the United States." Trump also aligned himself with other Islamophobic policies, such as surveillance of mosques and the establishment of a database to track all Muslim Americans. He exploited antisemitism. He wanted to change tax law to allow partisan politicking and fundraising in houses of worship. And he had shown, through endorsement of various pieces of legislation, a lack of understanding of the importance of careful balancing of rights in order to protect religious freedom for all, particularly when it came to LGBTQIA+ rights.

Many of us were alarmed about what a Trump presidency would mean for religious freedom and for our country, and our concerns were soon confirmed. On January 27, 2017, when I had been on the job just a few weeks, President Trump issued his Executive Order Protecting the Nation from Foreign Terrorist Entry into the United States, enacting his campaign promise of banning Muslims from coming to the United States. The Muslim travel ban included a suspension of visas for immigrants and nonimmigrants from seven Muslim-majority countries—Iran, Iraq, Libya, Somalia, Sudan, Syria, and Yemen—and a suspension of the refugee resettlement program, with a narrow exception in the future for those who face religious persecution *and* are considered a religious minority in that country.

The following week, speaking at the National Prayer Breakfast, President Trump said that he would "get rid of and totally destroy" the Johnson Amendment, the tax law that prevents nonprofit organizations from engaging in candidate campaigns for public office.

That was just during my first month on the job. Ever since, countless concerns have kept us on high alert. There have been expanding cracks in—if not the downright erosion of—the wall that separates church and state. There's been the resurgence of unapologetic and aggressive Christian nationalism in government, from the highest levels to local school boards; in the public square; and in American Christianity writ large.

But what alarmed me most were the white supremacists—armed with both guns and the violent and hateful ideology of Christian nationalism—threatening, terrorizing, and killing people in houses of worship. I think of the people who were shot to death at the gurdwara (Sikh temple) in Oak Creek, Wisconsin, in 2012. Of the worshippers gunned down at Mother Emanuel AME Church in Charleston in 2015. Of those killed at the Tree of Life Synagogue in Pittsburgh in 2018. I also think about the numerous bomb threats and acts of arson and vandalism at mosques, synagogues, churches, and other houses of worship.

I knew in my gut that the religious freedom community needed to respond to these attacks. In a pluralistic democracy, the ability to gather with like-minded believers for corporate worship in a church, mosque, synagogue, or any other house of worship is the most basic level of religious freedom. These attacks became the catalyst for me to join the movement to end Christian nationalism, which presents a clear, present, immediate, and ongoing threat to religious freedom.

OUR STORY

So in early 2019, my colleagues at BJC convened an interfaith table and then met with additional ecumenical partners to figure out what to do. The initiative was not in response to any specific event but a way to counter what we all perceived as a growing threat. Some of our interfaith partners quickly suggested that we focus our efforts to combat Christian nationalism *as Christians.* Our advocacy would be more effective, they told us, if it were a project led by Christians. Christians were in the best position to distinguish Christian nationalism from Christianity and to point out all the ways it distorts the gospel of Jesus Christ beyond recognition. Plus, they told us, not unkindly, that Christian nationalism was our problem—not theirs—to fix.

What I most remember about that initial meeting was that our interfaith allies did not feel safe in calling out Christian nationalism by name. There is currently a lot of risk in countering Christian nationalism, and they would be opening themselves up to danger in doing so. It was incumbent on us, the Christians in the room, to take on this challenge ourselves and confront this issue forcefully and on behalf of all religious groups.

One of the interfaith partners who was key in helping us discern our approach to ending Christian nationalism was Rabbi Jack Moline, an American Conservative rabbi and then president of Interfaith Alliance. Founded in 1994 to demonstrate that the Religious Right was not the only authentic voice of faith in this country, Interfaith Alliance is the only national interfaith organization dedicated to protecting the integrity of both religion and democracy in the United States. "The voice of pushback against Christian nationalism *has* to come from within Christendom," Rabbi Moline told us.

So we took Rabbi Moline and other interfaith colleagues' advice, and we launched Christians Against Christian Nationalism in July 2019. In naming the campaign, we felt it was important to name clearly what we were against. But we also knew it was just as important to name what we are *for*: religious freedom for all people. We crafted a statement of principles we thought could unite a large group of Christians who diverge on theology, ideology, politics, and many other lines of difference. That statement reads:

> *As Christians, our faith teaches us everyone is created in God's image and commands us to love one another. As Americans, we value our system of government and the good that can be accomplished in our constitutional democracy. Today, we are concerned about a persistent threat to both*

our religious communities and our democracy—Christian nationalism.

Christian nationalism seeks to merge Christian and American identities, distorting both the Christian faith and America's constitutional democracy. Christian nationalism demands Christianity be privileged by the State and implies that to be a good American, one must be Christian. It often overlaps with and provides cover for white supremacy and racial subjugation. We reject this damaging political ideology and invite our Christian brothers and sisters to join us in opposing this threat to our faith and to our nation.

As Christians, we are bound to Christ, not by citizenship, but by faith. We believe that:

> *People of all faiths and none have the right and responsibility to engage constructively in the public square.*
>
> *Patriotism does not require us to minimize our religious convictions.*
>
> *One's religious affiliation, or lack thereof, should be irrelevant to one's standing in the civic community.*
>
> *Government should not prefer one religion over another or religion over nonreligion.*
>
> *Religious instruction is best left to our houses of worship, other religious institutions and families.*
>
> *America's historic commitment to religious pluralism enables faith communities to live in*

civic harmony with one another without sacrificing our theological convictions.

Conflating religious authority with political authority is idolatrous and often leads to oppression of minority and other marginalized groups as well as the spiritual impoverishment of religion.

We must stand up to and speak out against Christian nationalism, especially when it inspires acts of violence and intimidation—including vandalism, bomb threats, arson, hate crimes, and attacks on houses of worship—against religious communities at home and abroad.

Whether we worship at a church, mosque, synagogue, or temple, America has no second-class faiths. All are equal under the US Constitution. As Christians, we must speak in one voice condemning Christian nationalism as a distortion of the gospel of Jesus and a threat to American democracy.

We asked Christians, both clergy and laity, to sign the statement. As of May 2024, more than 38,000 people have added their names and support to the effort to end Christian nationalism.

From the beginning, signers to the statement have agreed to have their names listed publicly on the website, along with their city, state, and whatever religious identification they chose. Some people simply write "Christian," others list a denomination, and others a specific church or other religious organization. There are signers from every congressional district in the country, representing urban, suburban, and rural communities, and signers span more than six dozen different Christian expressions. These principles of religious freedom for all have united a group of people across many lines of difference.

The statement was meant only as a beginning: a way to identify a group of people committed to working to end Christian nationalism. The campaign continues through work on the ground in local organizing projects across the country. Those of us who have signed the statement are building community with our neighbors across lines of difference. We are learning to understand how Christian nationalism is threatening our neighbors' freedom, and we are working to craft interventions to prevent that harm. My hope is that this book can connect you to local organizing projects in your community or, if one is not already started there, inspire you to begin one with the tools and resources available through the campaign.

YOUR STORY

What is your story in relationship to Christian nationalism? If you picked up this book, you're likely concerned about its rise and eager to figure out your role in ending it. As you read these steps and reflect on the Christian nationalism on display around you, you may feel anger, or despair, or worry.

You may find yourself thinking a lot about which elements of our common life you may have taken for granted. You might find yourself imagining the future, reflecting on what we all have at stake. What could happen if you talk to neighbors and friends and relatives about the danger of Christian nationalism? Or if you go with the flow and say nothing?

When my son was little, *The Lorax* was one of his favorite bedtime stories. The 1971 Dr. Seuss classic is a whimsical fable with a serious message about the dangers of unchecked consumerism and environmental exploitation. It's a warning about the perils of taking for granted our most precious resources, no matter what they are. Though Dr. Seuss's legacy has been complicated in recent years, most notably by his estate's decision to stop selling six of his books that contained racial and ethnic stereotypes, *The Lorax* shares important lessons for our time.

In the book, the resource is the Truffula tree, with colorful Truffula tufts that are used by an enterprising capitalist called the Once-ler to make a thneed—"It's a shirt! It's a glove! It's a hat! It's something everyone, everyone, everyone needs! And it can be yours for just $3.98!"

Soon the Once-ler has exploited the precious Truffula tufts, and only one Truffula tree remains. The impact on the community is immediate. The brown barbaloots have no Truffula fruits to eat and must find somewhere else to live. None of the swomee-swans can sing anymore because of the smog, and so they all fly away. The Humming-Fish's pond is so polluted they're forced to search for water that isn't so smeary. And as the story unfolds and the environmental devastation becomes shockingly apparent, the brightly colored illustrations become monochromatic and the land a postapocalyptic gray.

In interviews over the years, Theodor Seuss Geisel claimed that *The Lorax* was his personal favorite among the more than sixty books he published. "*The Lorax* came out of my being angry. The ecology books I'd read were dull," he said. "In *The Lorax*, I was out to attack what I think are evil things and let the chips fall where they might."

The environmental message of *The Lorax* is clear. Yet part of the book's genius is that it can speak to other issues as well. When I read *The Lorax* with my son, I suddenly heard it as a parable that speaks to our efforts to end Christian nationalism. Religious freedom is a precious resource. When it grows abundantly, it can support life in our pluralistic society and protect our democracy. But just like the Truffula trees, religious freedom easily can be taken for granted—something we notice only when it is threatened or denied.

The freedom to practice religion (or not) according to our individual consciences is beautiful and enticing, like those Truffula tufts. The temptation to use that freedom for political gain in pursuit of power can be hard to resist. Religious freedom is something that everyone, everyone, *everyone* needs. But when it is hoarded only for some people in some circumstances, then it is at risk of extinction for all people.

As a white Christian, I have tended for most of my life to think of our constitutional rights as limitless resources:

they have always been there and always will be secured for Americans by our founding generation for all time. But this faulty narrative speaks to the privileged place in society that I hold because I am a white Christian. Despite the founding myths that abound about the motivations of the Puritans to escape religious persecution and establish a colony based on principles of religious freedom, religious freedom has never been fully achieved—the few have always hoarded it at the expense of everyone.

Religious privilege is not religious freedom. The costs are borne most acutely by those who are oppressed and marginalized on account of race and their faith and religious exercise, though there is also a cost to those in power. Religion that relies on state control for protection and enforcement is not a flourishing faith that can be freely chosen. In other words, as long as Christian nationalism abounds, there cannot be religious freedom.

By the time the Once-ler is done exploiting the Truffula forests, all that's left of the life-giving resource is a stump imprinted with a single word: *unless.* As readers, we don't know what that means until the hero of the story—a young person—appears. Then we get it. "Unless someone like you cares a whole awful lot, nothing is going to get better. It's not."

We won't be able to secure our freedom for generations to come unless someone like you learns about it and tells or reminds other people about it. Unless you tend it and water it and nurture it. Unless you ensure nobody (including yourself) exploits it in ways that threaten the quality of life for everybody. Unless.

So in the pages that follow, we learn what Christian nationalism is, how it threatens our representative democracy and the Christian faith, and the way in which its pernicious and dangerous message has spread throughout the world. We learn what we all can and must do to stop it. And we listen to generous and wise thought partners who also are working to dismantle Christian nationalism. These include Christian allies, and they include kin from Islam, Judaism, secular humanism, atheism, and other religious and ethical traditions. Conversation partners in this book include people of color whose experiences allow them to see right through the twisted myths of white Christian nationalism—as well as the stories the United States likes to tell itself about its history—long before most white people do.

Christianity is not what unites us as Americans. Belonging in our society must never depend on how (or if) we worship, what we believe (or don't), or how we identify (or don't) religiously. If anyone tries to tell you that confronting Christian nationalism is somehow anti-Christian, do not believe them. Across this nation and throughout the world, many Christians are profoundly alarmed by Christian nationalist ideology—particularly the way it is used to perpetuate white supremacy—and want to ensure religious freedom for all people. Many Christians are also worried about how Christian faith itself would be cheapened and tamed were it to be blessed by the state. We must name Christian nationalism as the destructive ideology that it is, do whatever we can to end it, and repair the damage it has done to democracy as we aspire to a more liberative vision of religious freedom.

If all that is radical work, as the journalist suggested to me, then so be it. Let's explore how we can do that work together, as Christians and as people of all faith traditions and none, until defending faith freedom for all is commonplace.

This is an all-hands-on-deck moment in history. Let's get busy.

READ: You were called to freedom, brothers and sisters; only don't let this freedom be an opportunity to indulge your selfish impulses, but serve each other through love. All the Law has been fulfilled in a single statement: *Love your neighbor as yourself* (Gal. 5:13–14).

REFLECT AND ACT: We each have a role to play in working to end Christian nationalism. How do you come to this work? What events and experiences in your life have "radicalized" you to want to take action in your community? Write your own reflection on what brings you to this work of ending Christian nationalism.

ONE

Step One

Name and Understand the Threat
of Christian Nationalism

Like so many Americans, I watched the attack on the US Capitol on January 6, 2021, in horror. As a Christian, I watched in particular dismay as the mob incorporated Christian symbols, rituals, prayers, and Bible verses into their actions. Christian crosses and religious iconography were ubiquitous, and some of the rioters built impromptu gallows, presumably for Vice President Mike Pence or whomever else they were targeting, and decorated them with "Amen," "God Bless the USA," and "In God We Trust."

Flags flew everywhere, and many of them carried Christian images. There were red, white, and blue "Jesus 2020" banners and "Make America Godly Again" flags. There were Confederate flags—which some white Southern Christians have embraced for years—and the ecumenical Christian flag—a white flag with a blue field and a red cross—which a rioter carried onto the floor of the Senate while US Capitol Police drew their guns to keep the attackers out of the chambers. And there were more than a few white flags emblazoned with a single green evergreen tree and the words "Appeal to Heaven," which have become an emblem of Christian nationalism.

In one of the more unforgettable and bizarre scenes from the siege, a clutch of mostly male insurrectionists gathers on the Senate dais to offer a prayer. "Jesus Christ, we invoke your name!" one man begins in a video captured by the *New Yorker*. Shortly thereafter, the prayer session is commandeered by a bare-chested, bullhorn-wielding Jacob Chansley, a.k.a. the QAnon Shaman, with his red, white, and blue face paint and fur hat with black horns. "Let's all say a prayer in this sacred space," Chansley says before launching into a rambling monologue addressing a "divine, omniscient, omnipotent, and omnipresent creator God," whom he thanked for allowing the rioters to "exercise our rights, to allow us to send a message to all the tyrants, the communists, and the globalists that this is our nation, not theirs."

Christian nationalism was not the sole cause of or explanation for the events of January 6, but it played a vital role in the events leading up to the siege and provided a unifying ideology for many disparate groups that day. Christian nationalism imbued the violence with religious significance and added another layer of self-justification for the rioters' indefensible actions. The Christian language, symbols, and imagery also provided a common vocabulary for the perpetrators—one that carries great cultural significance and legitimacy.

If the QAnon Shaman represented the entirety of Christian nationalism, it would be easier to write off the movement as marginal and oddball. But Christian nationalism as an ideology can be embraced, in varying degrees, by anyone. And people who embrace Christian nationalism are wielding immense power—not just at riots but at the center of state and national government, on local school boards, and in churches and community organizations.

Christians who seek to follow the Christ revealed to us in the Bible must reckon with the expanded power and future trajectory of the Christian nationalist movement. While January 6 provides us with the most blatant examples of Christian nationalism in recent memory, Christian nationalism runs much wider, deeper, and longer than any one expression of it.

Christian nationalism is pernicious and insidious, and its influence in the United States is rising at an alarming rate. It is up to each of us to confront and call it out as the destructive ideology that it is and for the damage that it is causing our country—and the world. But in order to do that, we must first understand it. James Baldwin wrote, "Not everything that is faced can be changed; but nothing can be changed until it is faced." If we are to end Christian nationalism, we must first develop a better idea of the threat we are facing.

THE DEFINITION

Christian nationalism is a political ideology and cultural framework that seeks to fuse American and Christian identities. It suggests that "real" Americans are Christians and that "true" Christians hold a particular set of political beliefs. It seeks to create a society in which only this narrow subset of Americans is privileged by law and in societal practice.

You will notice that this definition is confined to Christian nationalism in the current US context. This is but one expression of a larger ideology of religious nationalism, which has been a recurrent problem throughout history—and still is around the world today. It helps to keep these connections in mind as we dive more specifically into the present problem we have in the United States. I will weave in references to the historical and global issue of religious nationalism where appropriate, but those topics are not the primary focus of this book.

Christian nationalism is a gross distortion of the Christian faith that I and so many others hold dear. It employs the language, symbols, and imagery of Christianity, and it might even appear to the casual observer to be authentic Christianity. But Christian nationalism merely uses the veneer of Christianity to advance its own aims. It points not to Jesus of Nazareth but to the nation, as conceived of by a dangerous political ideology, as the object of allegiance.

Christianity is a religious faith that follows Jesus and his gospel of love, and when Christian symbols and language are used to do that, we most likely are dealing with an authentic expression of Christianity. But when those same symbols and language accompany appeals to order and conformity, point the intended audience to the American flag, or compel political unity under a particular leader, we have moved into the territory of Christian nationalism.

Christian nationalism is the greatest threat to religious liberty in the United States today. Christian nationalism is antidemocratic, and it is a clear and present danger to our constitutional republic. Christian nationalism also poses an ongoing threat to the health and vitality of authentic Christian faith and practice in America.

Christian nationalism transfers religious devotion from worship of the divine to worship of earthly power. One of the ways it does this is by contending that America has been and should always be a distinctively "Christian" nation, from top to bottom—in its self-identity, interpretations of history, sacred symbols, cherished values, and public policies.

Christian nationalism is not a new problem. In terms of world history, we can date one of the first examples of Christian nationalism to the fourth century, when an emperor, Constantine, made Christianity the religion of his empire—and then used the military force of that empire for religious persecution in the name of Jesus. Prior to Constantine, Christianity was mostly a faith of the margins, interested less in garnering power in the nation than in spreading the good news of love and caring for those who were poor. Christians were much more likely to be persecuted for their faith than to wield political power to force their religion on others. Jesus eschewed political power in favor of a ministry aligned with those who were oppressed, marginalized, and otherwise harmed by that power. Jesus was eventually murdered by the empire for his radical message and acts of love.

After Constantine, the faith of Jesus morphed into the practice of European Christianity that used power to gain control by oppression. We should not overlook or underestimate the lasting impact this use of power to enforce and propagate Christianity has had on the integrity of the Christian faith. In other words, because of Christian nationalism, there has been an ever-widening gap between the teachings of Jesus and the religion of Christianity.

In the US context, Christian nationalism was present before the nation's inception. European invaders of this continent were armed with not just weapons and disease but also the blessing of the church in the form of the Doctrine of Discovery: a series of papal bulls that "justified" the seizure of land inhabited by people who were not Christians—all in the name of God.

Christian nationalism has ebbed and flowed throughout US history, with high tides at certain moments: in the generation after the founding (see the Naturalization Act of 1790, which restricted citizenship to "white persons"); the years preceding the Civil War (see the division of Christian denominations along North-South lines over the issue of slavery); the years of rapid population expansion due to immigration (see laws like the Chinese Exclusion Act of 1882); the years following Reconstruction (see the rapid growth of the Ku Klux Klan [KKK] in the early twentieth century); and the Red Scare of the 1950s (see the adoption of "In God We Trust" as a national motto and the addition of "under God" to the Pledge of Allegiance).

In all these instances, Christian nationalism flourished not only because it was a prevalent ideology but also because its adherents held political power and used it in law and policy, with actions taken and not taken. The same is true today: Christian nationalism is flourishing both because it is a pervasive ideology and because it is a well-funded political movement. Though it can be tempting to focus on the movement aspect of Christian nationalism, I think our efforts are better directed at dismantling the ideology—which is, admittedly, a much more difficult task.

MEASURING CHRISTIAN NATIONALISM

Christian nationalism as an ideology exerts its influence along a spectrum. I'd argue that we have all been shaped by it, to some degree. In their 2020 book *Taking Back America for God: Christian Nationalism in the United States*, sociologists Dr. Samuel Perry and Dr. Andrew Whitehead describe four different orientations toward Christian nationalism based on respondents' answers to six statements. They classify people who have fully embraced and advocate for Christian nationalist ideology as *ambassadors*; this turns out to be the smallest group, comprising less than 20 percent of the US population. At the opposite end of the spectrum from ambassadors are *rejecters*—people who, like me and maybe you, actively reject Christian nationalist ideology. We make up about 22 percent of the American populace.

As is true in much of US life, most Americans fall somewhere in the middle. Dr. Perry and Dr. Whitehead call the folks in this central band either *accommodators* of Christian nationalism (about 32 percent of Americans) or *resisters* (about 27 percent).

Using polling, Dr. Perry and Dr. Whitehead delineate each of these groups by how strongly they agree or disagree with the following statements:

1. "The federal government should declare the United States a Christian nation."
2. "The federal government should advocate Christian values."
3. "The federal government should enforce strict separation of church and state."
4. "The federal government should allow the display of religious symbols in public spaces."
5. "The success of the United States is part of God's plan."
6. "The federal government should allow prayer in public schools."

Ambassadors strongly agreed with each of the statements, and rejecters strongly disagreed with them (except the third one, which was reverse coded so that strong disagreement with this statement registered the same way strong agreement registered for the other statements). Accommodators and resisters fell somewhere in the middle.

In sharing this research with audiences over the past several years, I have often been asked a question that sounds something like this: "These statements are somewhat equivocal. It depends on what you mean by 'Christian values' to determine how I would respond to statement number two." Or "What exactly do you mean by 'prayer in public schools'? If it is government-led prayer, I'm against it, but I think students and teachers should still be able to pray." These are certainly valid critiques of the rubric, and I think some of that ambiguity is reflected in the more moderate positions that most respondents take as either resisters or accommodators.

There is often a latent defensiveness in the question, though. For the most part, the groups I meet with don't want to be associated with Christian nationalism and are afraid of being labeled as such. In doing the hard work of dismantling ideologies, labeling people definitively as "Christian nationalist" or "racist" is both counterproductive and inaccurate. We are better served by thinking of these as systemic problems that we can learn to recognize and then work to disengage from ourselves as we work with our communities to reject them. That's why throughout this book and in my public speeches and conversations, I choose to address "Christian nationalism" and not "Christian nationalists."

This method of measuring Christian nationalism as a scale has been repeated in other studies, including research from the Brookings Institution and Public Religion Research Institute (PRRI; February 2023) and Neighborly Faith (December 2023). While the questions used and the labels ascribed differ from study to study, the overall method of using survey questions to place respondents along a spectrum depending on how much they reject or embrace the assumptions, narratives, and stated goals of Christian nationalism has emerged as a consistent way to measure the prevalence of the ideology.

These studies also correlate how much one embraces Christian nationalism with our political opinions and attitudes. For instance, Dr. Perry and Dr. Whitehead have found through their research that Americans who embrace Christian nationalism are more likely to do the following:

- *Approve of authoritarian tactics such as demanding people show respect for national symbols and traditions*
- *Fear and distrust religious minorities, including Muslims, atheists, and Jewish people*
- *Condone police violence toward Black Americans and distrust accounts of racial inequality in the criminal justice system*
- *Believe racial inequality is due to the personal shortcomings of minority groups*

- *Report being "very uncomfortable" with both interracial marriage and transracial adoption*
- *Hold anti-immigrant views*
- *Fear refugees*
- *Oppose scientists and science education in schools*
- *Believe that men are better suited for all leadership roles while women are better suited to care for children and the home.*

In the 2023 PRRI/Brookings Institution study, the researchers identified five correlates of Christian nationalism: anti-Black racism, anti-immigrant views, antisemitic views, anti-Muslim views, and patriarchal understandings of gender roles. The more that a survey respondent embraced Christian nationalist views, the more likely they were to hold these other views. But a key finding showed that race, ethnicity, and religion made a difference as well. If someone was white and also an "adherent" to Christian nationalism, in the terms of that study, they were more likely to hold anti-Black racist positions than someone who was Black and an adherent to Christian nationalism.

A 2022 University of Maryland Critical Issues Poll regarding the constitutionality of declaring the United States a Christian nation found interesting data reflecting the latent white supremacy in Christian nationalism. White respondents who said they believed whites have faced more discrimination than other groups were most likely to embrace Christian nationalism.

"Christian nationalism, a belief that the United States was founded as a white, Christian nation and that there is no separation between church and state, is gaining steam on the right," professors Dr. Stella Rouse and Dr. Shibley Telhami, who helmed the poll, wrote in *Politico*. "Roughly 59 percent of all Americans who say white people have been discriminated against a lot more in the past five years favor declaring the US a Christian nation, compared to 38 percent of all Americans. White Republicans who said white people have been more discriminated against also favored a Christian nation (65 percent) by a slightly larger percentage than all Republicans (63 percent)."

Recent research also shows that Americans who hold strongly to myths about the United States' supposed Christian heritage tend "to draw rigid boundaries around ethnic and national group membership." Such boundaries tend to exclude Muslims as a group and to be less supportive of interracial family relationships. White people who embrace Christian nationalism use ethnic boundaries, prejudice, and perceived threats to justify harsher treatment—including the use of excessive force—against racial minorities. Research suggests that "adherence to Christian nationalism predicts that Americans will be more likely to believe that police treat blacks the same as whites and that police shoot blacks more often because blacks are more violent," Dr. Perry, Dr. Whitehead, and Joshua T. Davis wrote in the journal *Sociology of Race and Ethnicity*. The result is an unwillingness to acknowledge police discrimination and an increase in victim-blaming, catering to the racist idea that there is an inherent violence in Blackness that necessitates a violent response from law enforcement.

Despite the long-standing nature of Christian nationalism as an ideology, the currency of the term is still rather new. An extensive polling project by the Pew Research Center found that as recently as the fall of 2022, most Americans still were largely unfamiliar with the concept of Christian nationalism. More than half of those who participated in the poll had never heard of it. But the study found that those who had heard at least a little bit about Christian nationalism were five times more likely to hold an unfavorable opinion of it than to approve of it.

These responses show there is quite a bit of confusion about what Christian nationalism is. The study showed that Americans' views on Christian nationalism were wildly ambiguous depending on what they imagined when they heard the term. "Americans' views of Christian nationalism envision varying levels of Christian influence on the nation, ranging from strict theocratic rule to merely embracing moral values such as helping others," the Pew authors wrote.

What do we make of this public polling? Rather than seeing it as a cause for despair, I find a measure of hope buried in these statistics. In that ambivalence and ambiguity dwells an opportunity to educate and change hearts and minds. When people know more about Christian nationalism, they are much more likely to reject it than to embrace it. Clarity around what Christian nationalism is and the impact that it has on our and our neighbors' freedoms is an important first step to dismantling the ideology and its threat to democracy. Many of our friends, relatives, and colleagues who may be at risk of falling prey to Christian nationalist messaging are largely unfamiliar with the ideology. They need people in their lives—people like you and me—who can help them understand Christian nationalism well enough to reject it.

As we begin to talk with people about what Christian nationalism is—and isn't—we may find them returning to a popular version of the American founding story. Ending Christian nationalism will require us to directly confront a persistent myth: that the United States is a Christian nation.

THE MYTH

Christian nationalism requires a carefully curated, cherry-picked version of American history—one that perpetuates the myth of a Christian nation—to thrive. While there is no official or definitive version of this myth, it usually sounds something like this: *The United States was founded as a Christian nation, based on Christian principles, and has a special role to play in God's plan for humankind. If our leadership or national values stray from traditional Christianity, God will withdraw his blessings from the nation.*

The myth that the United States is a Christian nation is deeply embedded in culture. In the results of the 2022 poll referenced earlier, the Pew Research Center demonstrated just how widespread the narrative is. Six in ten Americans believe the founders of the United States originally intended it to be a Christian nation. One-third of respondents believe the United States presently *is* a Christian nation, and 45 percent of Americans said the United States *should* be a Christian nation.

Despite the pervasiveness of the myth, however, Americans are not of one mind about what it means. "Americans' view of *what it means to be a Christian nation* are wide-ranging and often ambiguous," the authors of the Pew study wrote. "To some, being a Christian nation implies Christian-based laws and governance. For others it means the subtle guidance of Christian beliefs and values in everyday life, or even simply a population with faith in something bigger." In other words, not all people who say the United States should be a Christian nation also think there should be no separation between church and state or that Christianity should become the official religion.

Digging deeper into the data, however, we do find some disturbing realities. The Pew survey found that nearly 80 percent of people who said the United States should be a Christian nation *also* say that the Bible should have at least some influence on US laws, with the majority of those people saying that when the Bible conflicts with the will of the people, the Bible should prevail. Taking the Bible seriously in one's own life as a Christian—using it as an authoritative and inspirational sacred text in one's faith—is much different from saying that the Bible should shape a country's laws. In a religiously pluralistic country, why should one religion's sacred text be privileged in lawmaking?

The PRRI/Brookings Institution study asked an even more pointed question about the Christian nation myth and to telling effect. The researchers asked respondents about agreement with this statement: "God intended America to be a new promised land where European Christians could create a society that could be an example to the rest of the world." The results showed a high correlation between agreement with this statement and Christian nationalism: 83 percent of *adherents* and 67 percent of *sympathizers* agreed with this statement.

While respondents' definitions of what constitutes a Christian nation vary, and while some of those definitions are more harmful than others, the very concept of a Christian nation is destructive. Let's look at how such a myth produces a distorted and biased telling of American history.

To exist, the Christian nation myth must downplay or ignore the role of Indigenous peoples, Black people, immigrants, religious minorities, people who don't claim a religious identity, and anyone else whose impact on and contributions to history might undercut the narrative that the United States is special because it was founded by and for white Christians. A telling of US history through the lens of the Christian nation myth begins with the so-called discovery of North America by Europeans. Such a narrative ignores the Indigenous peoples who had inhabited the land and had established complex and highly developed civilizations long before Christopher Columbus and his ilk stepped foot on these shores. The myth of a Christian nation idolizes the Puritans' quest for religious freedom in the "New World" but obscures the religious persecution they perpetrated against both the Indigenous peoples who were here when they arrived and those who arrived after them who didn't adhere to their strict doctrines. By claiming that God's providential hand has been at work throughout history, the myth suggests that God ordained the kidnapping of Africans and the system that legalized race-based slavery—a contention that I would think most people would reject.

The myth of a Christian nation is far more dangerous than simply being biased history. It undermines and contradicts the fundamental document on which our nation was founded: the US Constitution. The terms *Christian* and *Christianity* appear nowhere in the Constitution. In fact, the only reference to religion in the Constitution appears in Article VI, which states in part that "no religious Test shall ever be required as a Qualification to any Office or public Trust under the United States." Just a brief telling of the history of this clause will show that it was an intentional choice by the framers to reject a legal Christian nation.

When the Constitution was written and signed, most of the existing state constitutions or colonial charters contained some form of a religious test for holding public office. Such tests ranged from affirming a belief in Christianity (Maryland) and affirming specific doctrines such as the Trinity (Delaware) to blatantly disallowing anyone other than Protestants from holding public office (Georgia). So in 1787, many people believed that a civil government could and should enforce morality by requiring church attendance, personal statements of doctrinal beliefs, and financial support for churches. Thus, the "no religious Test" clause from Article VI of the Constitution was a radical departure from accepted norms. Those who attended the Constitutional Convention in Philadelphia during the summer of 1787 were all too familiar with religious tests, which tied a person's religious standing to political leadership and even citizenship. In the debates that preceded the ratification of the Constitution, Article VI was a source of tension. If Article VI were to be included, the signers realized, it would mean that someone other than a Protestant Christian could hold public office.

So our founding generation understood that religious diversity existed in America already and that it would only increase over time. In step 4, we will complicate some of this narrative, but the constitutional text remains. By rejecting any religious test for public office, the authors of the Constitution forged a new path for our burgeoning nation, one in which a person's civic duties would be independent of one's religious beliefs, practices, or identities. When Article VI was ratified, those who wanted a Christian nation lost the debate.

WHITE CHRISTIAN NATIONALISM

In addition to rewriting American history according to myth rather than fact, Christian nationalism is an expression of white supremacy. It overlaps with and provides cover for racial subjugation by creating and perpetuating a sense of cultural belonging in the United States only for certain people granted full citizenship at the founding of the nation: namely, native-born white Protestant Christian men.

Christian nationalism is pervasive—touching nearly every aspect of our culture—but in ways that are subtler and more easily overlooked than racism is. And Christian nationalism uses the social legitimacy of Christianity to make racism seem like an acceptable choice. Since the language of Christian nationalism is more coded than explicit racism, it often flies under the radar and is therefore hard to root out.

When I asked Dr. Anthea Butler how Christian nationalism provides cover for white supremacy, she paused before she answered. Dr. Butler is the author of *White Evangelical Racism*, a professor at the University of Pennsylvania, and one of the nation's leading historians of American and African American religion.

Her pause spoke volumes. "Do you see it that way?" I asked, starting to wonder what I was missing.

"Not exactly," Dr. Butler said. "I wouldn't say that Christian nationalism is a *cover* for white supremacy. What I would say is that people haven't been willing to admit how Christianity supports white supremacy. This is the thing: you can't really cover up something that's already there in plain sight."

Dr. Butler paused again to let the idea sink in. "Look. Through the history of this country—slavery, internment, forced resettlement on reservations—all those things had Christian connotations to them," she continued. "Christian nationalism is not so much a cover for white supremacy as it is basically a signpost on the door."

Dr. Butler noted that Christianity is the norm in this country, telling me that "whiteness, unfortunately, has become a norm as well. The founders might not have wanted Christianity to be the mainstage religion, but it ended up being that anyway."

Dr. Butler and her perspective showed me how I had internalized some of the assumptions of Christian nationalism in my approach to the topic. It is an uncomfortable truth that white Christianity has been infected with Christian nationalism for centuries, evident in the way the scriptures have been used to legitimate oppression. So for many BIPOC (Black, Indigenous, people of color) people, white Christianity, white supremacy, and Christian nationalism are cut from the same cloth.

Sure, the idea of the United States being established as a Christian nation may be a myth, Dr. Butler proceeded to say, but it's a "firm reality" in some people's minds. "It reminds me of that scripture that says the lie has become the truth. Well, this lie has become a particularly pervasive 'truth' . . . in this country."

The polling we looked at earlier shows how pervasive and sticky the Christian nation mythology is. I also think that acknowledging how people have absorbed the myth as truth helps explain the fragility that many white people exhibit when talking about how Christian nationalism and white supremacy are intertwined. Many white Christian Americans have bought the lie that American = Christian = white, even if we haven't realized it.

As my exchange with Dr. Butler shows, these truths are often more self-evident to people of color. Presiding Bishop Michael Curry of The Episcopal Church has spoken personally of his experience of racism and Christianity. "I am sixty-seven years old—been Black all those sixty-seven years—and I have known since childhood that the [Ku Klux] Klan professed to be Christian," Bishop Curry told me in one public conversation. "We grew up knowing that. So we knew there was an *unholy* conflation of Christianity and white supremacy, and it was often tinged with Americanism."

The idea that America is "God's favorite" borders on blasphemy and idolatry, he said, "That kind of nationalism is dangerous to civic health; it is dangerous to the health of Christianity. . . . When it gets going, it means if we're 'God's favorite,' and we're the 'chosen ones,' and we're in charge, then everybody else is secondary."

The idea of America's "chosenness" is particularly galling for Indigenous people in the United States, said Rt. Rev. Carol Gallagher, assistant bishop in the Episcopal Diocese of Massachusetts and an enrolled member of the Cherokee Nation. "[A]s an Indigenous person, I find it very hard to hear that phrase without understanding the price that was paid, not only in lives but land, people taken by disease, assumed to be 'less than,'" Rev. Gallagher said about the myth of American chosenness. "Native folks didn't get the right to vote until long after women got the right to vote. . . . Up until really the past thirty or forty years, Indigenous tribes have not even had the ability and the autonomy to even control their own lives and their own destiny."

One of the more horrendous chapters of American history that has been largely left out of textbooks is the forced removal—kidnapping, in many cases—of hundreds of thousands of Native American children from their families and communities. Threatening Native parents with fines or imprisonment, agents of the US government removed Native children from their homes and families and communities and placed them in boarding schools operated by the federal government and churches between 1869 and the 1960s.

There were more than 350 government-funded Indian boarding schools across the United States, most of them run by Christian church bodies, including Catholic, Methodist, Presbyterian, Episcopal, Baptist, Lutheran, and Unitarian denominations. While an accurate accounting of the true number of Indigenous children who were part of the boarding school system is unknown because the records are woefully incomplete, by 1900, there were 20,000 children in Indian boarding schools. By 1925, that number had tripled. By 1926, nearly 83 percent of school-age Native children were attending boarding schools. "Kill the Indian in him, and save the man," a saying coined by Richard Pratt, founder of the Carlisle Indian Industrial School in Carlisle, Pennsylvania—the flagship Native American boarding school in the nation from 1879 to 1918—was the guiding principle of assimilation.

According to the National Native American Boarding School Healing Coalition, thousands of Indigenous children over several generations were "taken to schools far away where they were punished for speaking their Native language, banned from acting in any way that might be seen to represent traditional or cultural practices, stripped of traditional clothing, hair, and personal belongings and behaviors reflective of their native culture. They suffered physical, sexual, cultural and spiritual abuse and neglect, and experienced treatment that in many cases constituted torture for speaking their Native languages. Many children never returned home and their fates have yet to be accounted for by the US government." The Canadian government has started to reckon with its history through reparations paid as part of lawsuit settlements. The US government only recently began to examine this history when Secretary of the Interior Deb Haaland announced the Federal Indian Boarding School Initiative in 2021. According to the Department of the Interior, the project is "a comprehensive effort to recognize the troubled legacy of federal Indian boarding school policies with the goal of addressing their intergenerational impact and to shed light on the traumas of the past."

"Many of our people, many of my mother's generation, were not allowed to speak their language," Rev. Gallagher said. "They were not allowed to do their traditions. The laws didn't come off the books in the state of Oklahoma and other places until well into the late 70s. You could be arrested and go to prison for practicing your traditional ways. And most of these people were also Christian. But various different seasons—Green Corn and other seasons that we celebrate as Cherokees—that was all done under the cover of darkness. I mean, what happens when people are sorely oppressed for generation after generation is—and there's a resilience in this—you go underground."

By operating many of the schools and lending their sacred mantle to their work, denominations worked hand in glove with the federal government in this mass program of family separation. White Christians must learn this history rather than shy away from it. "My grandfather grew up hearing, 'Kill the Indian, save the man.' That was our national policy," Rev. Gallagher continued. "There was a lot of killing. I mean, just death. If you go to Carlisle, you'll see the hundreds and hundreds of little crosses of children that just died, some of illness and many for just desperate loneliness and not being able to thrive."

What happened to Indigenous children in Indian boarding schools—the physical and psychological violence, the cultural genocide—mirrors what happened to enslaved peoples from Africa and elsewhere who were stripped of their cultural identity, language, customs, and religion.

The Bible has been used to give a divine imprimatur to some of humankind's worst behavior, whether slavery, genocide, or the inhumane treatment of non-Christians in the Americas. Through the Doctrine of Discovery, Spanish, English, and French colonizers viewed any land occupied by non-Christian Indigenous peoples as up for grabs for Christian settlers by divine right. "Christianity was right there being perverted to accommodate itself to what folk wanted to do to other folk, like Doctrine of Discovery," Bishop Curry said. "That has been a pattern."

Indeed, until we reckon with the fact that Christianity has been deployed as a weapon to dehumanize people throughout history, we will not see clearly the ways it is being used to do so today.

"What is it about Christianity that allows this kind of stuff to happen?" Dr. Butler asked me. "What if the problem is inherent not just in Christian nationalism, which it obviously is, but in Christianity itself? Not in Jesus and his teachings but in the religion that grew out of the man and his way and what he taught?"

THE DANGER

In its most dangerous form, Christian nationalism inspires acts of intimidation and physical violence—including vandalism, bomb threats, arson, hate crimes, attacks on places of worship, and even murders—against religious communities in the United States and abroad. It also threatens the physical safety of Americans in their communities and homes, as well as in the halls of political power.

As I mentioned in the introduction, I became a leader in the fight against Christian nationalism because of my increasing alarm about the physical violence it inspires in our nation's places of worship. All Americans should be safe when they gather in churches, mosques, synagogues, and elsewhere for corporate worship. In a society where mass shootings are horrifyingly commonplace, the massacre at Mother Emanuel AME Church in Charleston, South Carolina, on June 17, 2015, dealt a particularly heavy blow to our collective consciousness.

On that awful day, a twenty-one-year-old white man drove several hours to the historic Black church known as Mother Emanuel, where he joined a small group of worshippers meeting for a Bible study and prayer for an hour. Then he stood up, pulled a gun out of his fanny pack, aimed it at an eighty-seven-year-old woman, and began to shoot. He murdered Rev. Sharonda Coleman-Singleton, Cynthia Graham Hurd, Susie J. Jackson, Ethel Lee Lance, Rev. DePayne Middleton-Doctor, Rev. Clementa Pinckney, Tywanza Kibwe Diop Sanders, Rev. Daniel Lee Simmons Sr., and Myra Singleton Quarles Thompson.

His motive? "You rape our women, and you're taking over our country. And you have to go," is what he told his victims before opening fire. The gunman, Dylann Roof, admits to— brags about, in fact—being motivated by racist and white supremacist ideas.

Often missing from the coverage of the Mother Emanuel murders is how inextricably linked Roof's racist ideology was to his twisted view of Christianity. At the time of the massacre, he reportedly was a member in good standing at a different Christian church—St. Paul's Lutheran Church in

Columbia, South Carolina. The congregation in which he was baptized and grew up regularly attending Sunday school is part of the Evangelical Lutheran Church in America, one of the more progressive mainline Protestant denominations in the nation and decidedly unlike its more conservative Southern evangelical cousins.

Roof's prison journals are filled with Christian images and references—including a drawing of a white Jesus stepping out of the tomb—alongside racist, antisemitic, and Islamophobic screeds. Roof writes at length and without a whisper of remorse about how integral white supremacy is to his understanding of Christianity. He calls on white Christians to transform their religion. "Christianity doesn't have to be this weak, feeble, cowardly religion," he writes. "There is plenty of evidence to indicate that Christianity can be a warrior's religion."

Roof was convicted in December 2016 of all thirty-three federal charges against him, including twelve counts of a hate crime and twelve counts of violating a person's freedom of religion. In January 2017, he was sentenced to death. At Roof's sentencing hearing, prosecutors read a passage from his prison journal into the court record: "I would like to make it crystal clear, I do not regret what I did. I am not sorry."

Another mass shooting—the killing of shoppers inside a supermarket in a predominantly Black neighborhood of Buffalo, New York, on May 14, 2022—is perhaps the most salient example among such horrific events of the word *Christian* in Christian nationalism signaling identity, not religion. Ten people were murdered: Celestine Chaney, Roberta A. Drury, Andre Mackniel, Katherine Massey, Margus D. Morrison, Heyward Patterson, Aaron Salter Jr., Geraldine Talley, Ruth Whitfield, and Pearl Young. All were Black. The shooter, eighteen-year-old Payton Gendron, was a white supremacist who identified with Christian nationalism but not as a Christian.

In a 180-page manifesto, in which he expounds on the virulently racist "great replacement" conspiracy theory, Gendron also explains that he isn't a Christian but tries to "believe in and live out Christian values." The preservation of whiteness motivated him to commit these heinous murders, part of which he live streamed on the Twitch platform. A central aspect to "white culture," as he understands it, is the Christian religion. For Gendron, living out "Christian values" is entirely compatible with racism, antisemitism, and the indiscriminate murder of Black people.

Sociologist Dr. Samuel Perry describes Gendron's worldview as centering on "culture and Christian values, whatever that means. And it's connected to Whiteness and nationality." Christian nationalism is the best explanation for this disconnect—how "Christian values" are used as a kind of divine imprimatur for white supremacy and twisted ideologies, such as the great replacement theory.

In their book *The Flag and the Cross: White Christian Nationalism and the Threat to American Democracy*, Dr. Perry and Dr. Philip Gorski reveal polling data to back up this seemingly inexplicable disconnect. In a recent survey, more than 15 percent of those who checked the box as "Christian" and nearly 19 percent of those who specifically claimed to be "born again" or "evangelical" also said they belonged to a non-Christian religion or were secular. Like Gendron, such respondents want to claim the identity of Christianity but not necessarily subscribe to its practices and core beliefs, such as the authoritative life, death, and resurrection of Jesus the Christ, who told us to love our neighbors as ourselves.

The 2022 University of Maryland Critical Issues Poll further demonstrated the disconnect between biblical Christianity and the Christian nation myth, which undergirds Christian nationalism and also undermines the Constitution. According to the poll, a large majority of all Americans (70 percent) said that the US Constitution would not allow the United States to be declared a Christian nation, and 62 percent of all Americans would oppose such a declaration. While both are resounding majorities, it is striking that having previously said such a declaration would be unconstitutional (57 percent), a majority of Republican voters (61 percent) *still* said they would support such a declaration. With regard to the age of the respondents, the poll found more support for declaring the United States a Christian nation among the silent generation (roughly those born in the mid-1920s through the mid-1940s) and baby boomers (those born between the end of World War II and the mid-1960s) and less support among younger people—even among young Republicans—for such a declaration.

While Christian nationalism is hardly a new phenomenon in the United States, more and more people have started talking about it while using that terminology in recent years. A Google trend report of searches for *Christian nationalism* since 2012 shows interest increasing slowly over the past decade, with a spike in 2022 that outpaced the nine previous years combined. Three of the biggest spikes in online searches for *Christian nationalism* during those years were January 2021, July 2022, and October 2022. The most likely causes for these three spikes were the attack on the US Capitol on January 6, 2021; US Congresswoman Marjorie Taylor Greene's declaration in the summer of 2022 that she is a proud Christian nationalist and that the Republican Party should be the party of Christian nationalism; and several politicians during the 2022 midterm elections using Christian nationalism as part of their campaign strategies.

Understanding both the political ideology and cultural framework of Christian nationalism is essential to dismantling white supremacy and preserving true religious freedom for all. In the United States, we have let Christian nationalism fester for too long.

Calling out and criticizing the dangers of Christian nationalism is not anti-Christian. Indeed, it is our very commitment to Christian values—centrally, love—that leads many of us to this work. Our love of our neighbors naturally should include a commitment to protect their rights of citizenship and equal belonging regardless of which religion they practice—or whether they practice any religion at all.

Many of us who call ourselves Christians have seen how Christian nationalism has grossly distorted our faith and the teachings of Jesus. As we seek to distinguish authentic versions of our faith from this idolatrous ideology, our next step to ending Christian nationalism is grounding ourselves in the central beliefs of our faith.

READ: Again you have heard that it was said to those who lived long ago: *Don't make a false solemn pledge, but you should follow through on what you have pledged to the Lord.* But I say to you that you must not pledge at all. You must not pledge by heaven, because it's God's throne. You must not pledge by the earth, because it's God's footstool. You must not pledge by Jerusalem, because it's the city of the great king. And you must not pledge by your head, because you can't turn one hair white or black. Let your *yes* mean yes, and your *no* mean no. Anything more than this comes from the evil one (Matt. 5:33–37).

REFLECT AND ACT: How would you define and describe Christian nationalism to your neighbor? How and where do you see the myth that the United States is a Christian nation popping up in conversation and culture? What, if anything, do you find surprising in the studies cited here? What makes you uncomfortable? Explore this step and the resources cited so you can develop a better sense of Christian nationalism in order to be able to talk about it with others.

TWO

Step Two

Ground Yourself in God's Love

Julie Greenfield is a self-described lifelong conservative Christian. "I believe the Bible is the inspired word of God, and I used to support the Religious Right," Greenfield told me in a recent conversation. "I've been a born-again Christian for fifty years, so you might think I would actually be a Christian nationalist, but I'm not. I'm strongly against it. It's my passion to end Christian nationalism because I believe it promotes and teaches heresy, which in the end are snuffing out true Christianity—or biblical Christianity—in America."

Having read about the Christians Against Christian Nationalism campaign and my testimony before Congress about the threat of Christian nationalism, Greenfield got in touch with me out of the blue. Until 2015, Greenfield and her husband, Jack, had always voted Republican straight down the ballot. In fact, if Jeb Bush had secured the Republican nomination for president in 2016, they happily would have voted for him. But then Trump became the nominee.

"We were horrified," Greenfield said. "We were doubly horrified that the Christian, evangelical, conservative community endorsed him. That was our 'aha' moment. We just started to basically hit our heads against the wall. 'How could this be? Why would our Christian community support such a man?'"

For years, the Greenfields had been busy raising their children and attending theologically conservative churches. They focused on God's love as they lived out their faith, and they steered clear of bringing partisan politics into church. They received newsletters from various right-wing political organizations and often used conservative voting guides to help them make decisions before heading to the polls. But they spent most of their energies trying to raise loving children, follow Jesus, and serve their community and their church.

As the hostility on Fox News and other right-wing media outlets ramped up, the Greenfields decided to opt out. In hindsight, Greenfield said, she realized "Christian nationalism is what the Religious Right has been teaching for fifty years. Since the 1980s, it's been *drip, drip, drip, drip* into American Christianity. But Christian nationalism is a human, earthly political movement that has a veneer of

Christianity around it. Its tenets are actually heresy. They have nothing to do with who the biblical Jesus is or with biblical Christianity. Exposing that is what inspires me."

Ending Christian nationalism is a political necessity, but as Julie Greenfield's story shows, it's more than that. For Julie and for me and for many people, it is a spiritual imperative. To do this vital and difficult work, we must ground ourselves in the core values and beliefs of Christianity. When facing a clear and present threat like Christian nationalism, we can't afford *not* to call on the faith that sustains us.

There are many different ways to live out the Christian faith. Christian practice and thought have taken thousands of diverse expressions throughout time and geography. Sometimes those expressions are marked by denominational identity, although tremendous variation exists within any given denomination. Take my denominational identity as a Baptist. According to the Baptist World Alliance, fifty-one million people living in 128 countries and territories around the world today claim a Baptist identity. The Association of Statisticians of American Religious Bodies counts fifty-seven different types of Baptist bodies or conventions in the United States today. And even those bodies cannot claim to speak for each believer. If this is true of Baptists, we can safely say that no one set of words can describe what it means to be a Christian.

Still, some core concepts—such as human freedom, love, and equality—that are made manifest in the person of Jesus Christ are foundational to the faith that so many people around the world hold dear. Our Christian faith teaches us, for example, that everyone is created in God's image. The concept of *imago Dei* is found in the very first chapter of Genesis, in the first creation story, and in the way God created humans in God's image (Gen. 1:26–27).

And what is one of the first things those humans did? They disobeyed God. God could have created Mary Poppins–like robots: practically perfect in every way. But God didn't do that. God created humans as free beings: free to say yes and free to say no and free to say nothing at all.

With freedom, though, comes responsibility and account-ability. The humans in the creation story also suffered the consequences of the decisions they made with their freedom. Despite all our imperfections and mistakes, we are all chil-dren of God. Recognizing the divine image in each person is the first step to loving our neighbor.

If I had to sum up Christianity in one word, that word would be *love*. When a lawyer questions Jesus about the greatest commandment, Jesus first quotes the Torah: Deuter-onomy's instruction to "love the Lord your God with all your heart, with all your being, and with all your mind." And then Jesus adds a twist, another way to see that commandment in our earthly context: "You must love your neighbor as you love yourself." On these two commandments, Jesus says, "all the Law and the Prophets depend" (Matt. 22:37–40).

The gospel—or "good news"—of love recurs throughout the life and teachings of Jesus and features most prominently in the Gospel of John. Perhaps the most memorized Bible verse in our era is John 3:16: "God so loved the world that he gave his only Son, so that everyone who believes in him won't perish but will have eternal life." Jesus taught us that just as God showed love for us, we are to show love for God by loving one another (John 15:12). Jesus told his followers, "This is how everyone will know that you are my disciples, when you love each other" (John 13:35). The chorus of one of the most popular hymns written in the past century is "And they'll know we are Christians by our love."

We sing those words but know that far too often, we fail to live up to them. The rise of Christian nationalism seems to have ushered in an era of breathtaking mean-spiritedness among many who identify as Christian. In this step, we ask some hard questions about why that is the case.

WHICH JESUS?

"Which Jesus do you serve? Which Jesus do you believe in?" Those are questions from Rev. Dr. Jonathan C. "Jay" Augustine, senior pastor of St. Joseph AME Church in Durham, North Carolina. Dr. Augustine is also a law professor at North Carolina Central University and a missional strategist with the Duke Center for Reconciliation. He says that, when considering the different ways Black and white American Christians understand religions freedom, he often asks those questions—sometimes from the pulpit.

While interviewing Dr. Augustine for an episode of the podcast I cohost, *Respecting Religion*, I was struck by many of his remarks, and they have stayed with me. He didn't mince words about what he sees happening in American Christianity. "The Jesus that I serve as a Christian minister is one who believes in equality of all, one who advocated for equality of all, one who certainly was egalitarian in practice, one who embraced those who were pushed to the margins," he said.

"There've been two very different sides of Christianity, if you will, at least for the last forty years in the United States of America," said Dr. Augustine. "Over the course of the last few years in particular, as we have seen a narrative called 'Make America Great Again,' I think there's been a great deal of buyer's remorse. . . . Some people have said, quite frankly, 'This is not what I signed up for, this level of polarization, this level of "otherism," this level of racial and ethnic enmity.'"

Indeed, in the United States these days, there appear to be at least two competing ideas of what Christianity should be. One says Christianity is as American as apple pie, that the terms *Christian* and *American* are synonymous, and that every American should be a Christian because that's what the founders intended. America was, is, and always should be a Christian nation, they say—and many are willing to use their guns to enforce or defend that idea.

The other version says Christianity is a way of living based on the teachings of a first-century Jewish man: Jesus, a carpenter and a teacher from Judea. This version claims that Jesus taught his motley band of followers to love radically, including to love one's enemies; to care for those who are poor, sick, widowed, orphaned, and on the margins; and to visit prisoners. Jesus gave his life for humanity and taught that the first shall be last and the last shall be first.

Jesus's actions—such as feeding those who were hungry, healing those who were sick, and centering women and children in a culture where they weren't valued—were inherently political, according to Rev. Dr. Jacqui Lewis, the senior minister of Middle Church in New York City. Christians follow the way of the "Afro-Semitic *pobrecito*—the poor one—born in Bethlehem, where the cows eat; raised in Nazareth, which is Palestine—raised in a place where 'nothing good comes from,'" Dr. Lewis said during a 2021 BJC event. Jesus was an outsider who stood in opposition to empire. At points during his thirty-three years on earth, Jesus experienced homelessness and was a refugee. "To follow in the way of that one is to follow in the narrow place . . . that slogs off for us any sense of privilege and power, except the kind that comes from being last, except the kind that comes from standing in solidarity with the people who Jesus stood in solidarity with: the outsiders, the disenfranchised, the tax collectors, the women, the sinners," Dr. Lewis said.

Christian nationalism, then, is a gross distortion of Christianity, one that bears little resemblance to anything Jesus said or taught. It strays far from the theologies that have been central to Christianity for two millennia. "I see it as a conflation of cross and country that says there is a dominant power narrative that is oftentimes rooted in white Anglo-Saxon Protestant practices," Dr. Augustine told me. "And if you are not within that category, then . . . you are devalued or valued as less than those who are, and it's a question of where you fit in"—or don't.

Because Christian nationalism is a debasement of the most foundational teachings of Christ and Christianity—chiefly, that we are all God's children and that we should love each other as Jesus loved us, which was radically, sacrificially, and unconditionally—it's crucial for Christians to confront and dismantle it.

IDOL WORDS

Christian nationalism replaces the gospel of love with a false idol of power. An idol is anything that is not God and that claims our total allegiance, devotion, and worship. In her book *Amazing Grace: A Vocabulary of Faith*, Kathleen Norris writes, "Idolatry makes love impossible." The world puts up many barriers to love, including prejudice, racism, discrimination, violence, and inequality. The common denominator among these barriers is named in the Ten Commandments in the admonition against idolatry. False idols detract from the love of God, neighbor, and self, leading to utter ruin.

Idols might include money, guns, and nation. Dr. Andrew Whitehead, a sociologist and a Christian, suggests that Christian nationalism bows to three idols in particular: power, fear, and violence. In his book *American Idolatry: How Christian Nationalism Betrays the Gospel and Threatens the Church,* Dr. Whitehead says that sometimes idol worship might look like true religion, but it is actually a faux faith—a cultural framework that distorts our religion into an ethnonational identity. White Christian nationalism twists and mangles God's love into an ideology that subjugates and dehumanizes our neighbors, creates an "us versus them" narrative, and threatens their very existence—and ours.

In January 2021, just a few weeks after the attack on the Capitol, I spoke with Bishop Elizabeth Eaton of the Evangelical Lutheran Church in America and Presiding Bishop Michael Curry of The Episcopal Church during a webinar open to the public. We talked about the theological problems with Christian nationalism. Bishop Eaton identified Christian nationalism's tendency toward idolatry as a "primary problem." She explained, "Since the beginning of the Christian movement, one of the earliest confessions of faith was 'Jesus is Lord,' which was seen as a direct threat to, at that time, the Roman Empire and the emperor—a threat to the state. Christians faced persecution because they declared that their primary allegiance was not to any temporal or secular government, but it was to the Lord." For Lutherans, she said, Christian nationalism is "a perversion of how we understand that we are in fact citizens with the saints and not citizens primarily or ultimately of any one temporal government."

Bishop Curry described Christian nationalism as "a violation of Christianity based on Jesus Christ as Lord from the very beginning." He said, "If you look at the history of Christianity, when it has gone astray, whether it is in support of slavery or silence in the midst of evil against any people . . . there is a consistent pattern that Jesus of

Nazareth—his actual teachings, his example, his spirit, the Sermon on the Mount, Matthew 25, the parable of the sheep and goats, the Good Samaritan—that Jesus of Nazareth gets moved aside and suppressed for a broad, ambiguous 'Christ' figure who can be adapted to any cultural context or adapted to anybody's whims." He explained that we get into dangerous waters when Jesus is compromised: "Whether it has been theological ways of being comfortable with apartheid, whether it was in the Nazi Church, whether it has been white supremacist Christianity."

When love is absent, hate moves in, and it festers and kills. Recognizing the idols that Christian nationalism worships helps us to clear the way for love. When we let go of idols, we make space for love. And in both our private lives and the public square, we live out love for others by safeguarding their freedom as we would our own.

WHITE SUPREMACY IS NOT LOVE

Progressive Christians and conservative Christians in America have become ideologically entrenched and pitted against each other. Given the perils of white Christian nationalism, it's essential for us to work together to combat racism. But we also need to be clear what values we want to align our faith with and which ones are beyond the pale.

"We—speaking as a white Christian—have inherited a Christianity that was by design built to be compatible with slavery, segregation, and white supremacy," said Dr. Robert

P. Jones, founding chief executive officer of PRRI and author of *The Hidden Roots of White Supremacy and the Path to a Shared American Future* and *White Too Long: The Legacy of White Supremacy in American Christianity*. White Christians need to reckon honestly with how we have historically benefited from systemic racism if we want to "rescue the faith," Dr. Jones said during a 2020 BJC event as he was interviewed by Adelle Banks, a senior correspondent for Religion News Service. "We've inherited that. It's in the DNA," he said. "We really do have to find the will and conviction to have the hard conversations, to tell the stories, to really rescue the faith from the distortions that history has brought forward to us."

Part of my own ongoing work of reckoning with whiteness is exploring my Christian roots among the Southern Baptists—a denomination that was formed to defend and preserve chattel slavery and that only recently began speaking openly about its racist origins. Although I haven't identified as a Southern Baptist for more than thirty years, those were the waters of faith into which I was baptized.

If you are a white Christian, you must be willing to examine your complicity in institutional racism. No matter which denomination or tradition we belong to, we must work to reconstruct a theology that is on the side of the enslaved, disenfranchised, and powerless—one that is closer to what Jesus actually taught than to the distorted, funhouse-mirror version of "Christian" theology espoused by Christian nationalism.

Virulent and public white supremacists such as members of the KKK or the Proud Boys might allow many white Christians to imagine we're not part of the "real" problem of racism, but if so, we are just kidding ourselves. We're all part of systemic injustices, including racism. "This is not just a white evangelical problem," Dr. Jones said. "This is a white Catholic problem, and this is a white mainline Protestant problem."

PRRI research showed that white Christians—Catholics, mainline Protestants, and evangelicals—are twice as likely as religiously unaffiliated white Americans to call the killing of Black men by police "isolated incidents and not part of a broader pattern," which is an indication of an "inability to see structural racism," Dr. Jones said. "On these kind of questions—the killing of unarmed African American men by police, the display of the Confederate flag—who is closer to African Americans? It is not white Christians. It is whites who are not Christian and the religiously unaffiliated," he said.

Dr. Jones's findings indicate that something in white Christianity itself is perpetuating racism. White Christians have a choice here: we can be offended by this assertion and reject the challenge, or we can assume a stance of humble curiosity. We can ask, how is our religion contributing to racist attitudes that bear no resemblance to the gospel?

The roots run very deep. When we first launched the Christians Against Christian Nationalism campaign, I talked with Dr. Jemar Tisby, historian and best-selling author of

The Color of Compromise: The Truth About the American Church's Complicity in Racism, for a podcast about the connections between racism and Christian nationalism. Dr. Tisby recounted the history of slave codes, by which race-based slavery became legal in what would become the United States. It's a legal history dating to 1667 and the Assembly in the Colony of Virginia. Virginia was an Anglican colony, and the assembly was composed exclusively of white Anglican men. Race-based chattel slavery had been in Virginia by this point for decades. But the Anglican church was also busy baptizing new believers.

Here's where the power of the state and the power of the church came into conflict. How did these Virginian Christian men—who were also political leaders—choose to reconcile the competing interests of church and state? "They made a law that said baptism would not free an enslaved Native American or any person of African descent or mixed-race background," Dr. Tisby noted. These religiopolitical leaders sacrificed their theology in favor of their thirst for political power. It was a choice that came at the expense of human beings, of fellow children of God. They chose to be oppressors rather than liberators, creating a "dichotomy between a person's spiritual well-being and their physical or material well-being, which is an argument that persists into the twenty-first century," Dr. Tisby said. He noted that some people tend to think they simply need to convert people to make the world a better place without working toward systemic change.

It's a choice, of course, that too many Christians have continued to make for hundreds of years: aligning themselves with the status quo, with empire, no matter the cost to their neighbors. Reflect for a moment about what that choice has meant for our society, for our country, today. Think about how racism has destroyed countless lives over the centuries, torn families apart, and diminished the humanity of us all. Consider how racism continues to divide and oppress so many. Look at how our white supremacy has worked against God's plan for equality and love.

MAKE BABYLON GREAT AGAIN?

Our love of God reminds us of Jesus's command: "Give to Caesar what belongs to Caesar and to God what belongs to God" (Mark 12:17). Clarity about our allegiance is critical, lest we confuse political leadership with religious authority. The merging of religious and political identity in Christian nationalism "makes God a captive and domesticates God," said Rev. Dr. Walter Brueggemann, one of the most influential Christian theologians and scholars of our time, when I spoke with him about the theological problems with Christian nationalism for a podcast. "When God is domesticated, it really leaves us without hope," Dr. Brueggemann told me in that conversation. "What's going on in US politics—it is essentially a politics of despair, in which we believe that nothing radically good can happen, and therefore it is a scramble to get as many of the marbles in our pocket before the game ends. But that's a no-win strategy because in the long run, it diminishes everyone's life—those who are on top of the heap and those who are underneath them."

I was struck at the time by Dr. Brueggemann's profound observation of our political life and the role that faith plays and could play if we were to dismantle Christian nationalism. By merging the almighty power of God with the earthly power of the state, we reduce the sacred to the secular. We turn God into a mascot for the state.

In talking with him, it became clear how Christian nationalism puts God in a small box that can be controlled and understood through a lens of a certain national identity. We see this idea of nationalism being merged with religious identity—or even being at odds with certain religious identities—throughout the Bible. And the work of confronting the perpetrators of those ideas has often been done by prophets.

"The prophetic tradition is a great nemesis [of religious nationalism]," Dr. Brueggemann said, noting that King Nebuchadnezzar wanted to "make Babylon great again," but his hubris in trying to do so caused the prompt downfall of the Babylonian empire. "So the story of arrogant power that imagines that it is religiously legitimated runs all through the Old Testament. And time after time, such a hoax turns out to be unsustainable because God's way in the world finally will not tolerate that. So it becomes a question in the United States, with our idolatrous religious ideology: how long is this enterprise sustainable in the real world where God is sovereign?"

He noted that question doesn't have an easy answer, but it must be entertained. It's clear to me that when an empire claims for itself the mantle of sacred legitimacy, Christians must confront it by speaking truth to power. This is especially true when Christians are benefiting from the empire's power.

"Empires and monopolies of power generally depend on very anemic gods who do not do anything except smile and bless," he said. "And obviously the God to whom the prophets bear witness is not an anemic god." Dr. Brueggemann pointed out that the status quo prefers gods that do nothing but legitimize the way things are. "So it really is a 'God versus god' issue—a robust true God versus false anemic gods," he said, noting that those issues can immediately descend into political and economic matters.

He noted that Good Friday—the crucifixion of Jesus Christ by state authorities—was the pinnacle of power of the Roman Empire, and the resurrection of Christ on Easter Sunday shows that earthly power was superseded by God's power. "And what the crucifixion/resurrection narrative bears witness to is that the presumption of any nation or any empire has its limits and finally cannot defeat God's intention for an alternative way in the world," Dr. Brueggemann said. "So I see the confession of Easter as being pivotal for political practice in the world because it says that God's will for life and for well-being finally is the truth of the world, and when we sign on for that we sign on for all kinds of possibilities that the nation—or the empire—does not want to entertain." He encouraged me to start with an understanding of what the God of the gospel is really like as we develop our next steps.

"I think we need many strategies," Dr. Brueggemann said, as we talked about how to respond to Christian nationalism and speak truth to power. "I don't think there's an obvious right way to do that. But I think we have to be working at the reform of the church so that the church community really becomes a place of truth-speaking rather than privatized, other-worldly stuff. I think we have to be politically active. I think we have to be on the streets in protest. I think we have to be performing the truth that is entrusted to us in every way that we have the courage to do."

He said the freedom of the gospel permits us to imagine hope and possibility for fashioning new policies and relationships beyond any one person's vested interest. "So that kind of hope is a peculiar gift of the gospel to our political conversation."

PURSUING TRUTH AND DISMANTLING MYTHS

Believing that a truth has been entrusted to us, as Dr. Brueggemann so aptly notes, means being brave enough to confront the myths around us that masquerade as truth.

Bishop Michael Curry offers three steps to confronting Christian nationalism and its insidious lie that God favors some people and groups over others. They include

(1) re-centering Christianity on the teachings and example of Jesus; (2) calling on our common humanity; and (3) rebuilding relationships between people across political, racial, and religious differences.

"We are all children of God made in God's image and likeness, and that means . . . we are related to each other," Bishop Curry said. He added that we need to build and rebuild relationships intentionally across differences. "Get to know them, spend some time with them, let that become a personal value for your life, and then maybe we can begin to chip away" at bias and prejudice, Curry said. "We must speak up and show up when something happens against our Jewish brothers and sisters, against our Muslim, our Sikh brothers and sisters," he said. "We must stand publicly for things that don't give us any advantage . . . [and] advocate in the public sphere for what is just and kind and decent and humane."

People need to see a different version of Christianity and not only the distorted version that Christian nationalism showcases. We must reclaim our faith. "It's that simple," Bishop Curry said. "We've got to speak up and stand up."

It is precisely that reasoning that caused Julie Greenfield, whom you met at the beginning of this step, to begin speaking out against Christian nationalism. There are many components of Christian nationalism that make it a heresy, Greenfield told me, but the most egregious is that "God is behind what the Religious Right is doing, what the Republican Party is doing, what the far right is doing. 'God is at work,' they say. They might not like all of Trump's behavior, but despite that, 'God is at work.'"

Greenfield shook her head. "Jesus would never use politics to build his kingdom," she said. "Jesus never wanted to leverage human institutions or human political leaders to accomplish his purposes. He said, 'My kingdom is not of this world' and 'my kingdom is within you.' The Bible says our citizenship is in heaven."

Greenfield would like to hear more pastors explicitly condemn Christian nationalism. "We know many pastors who preach that we should live and love like Jesus, but they stop there," she said. "They don't say that what the Religious Right says—that God wants America to be Christian politically and wants Christians to take control of America—is a heresy. They need to say it, and lay people need to say it too."

I am grateful for the prophetic preachers and lay leaders—from across the centuries and in our modern times—who are grappling with how Christian nationalism distorts the gospel of Jesus. In the next step, we will focus on one specific area that should unite all people in opposing Christian nationalism: denouncing and trying to prevent physical violence and threats of violence.

READ: Dear friends, let's love each other, because love is from God, and everyone who loves is born from God and knows God. The person who doesn't love does not know God, because God is love (1 John 4:7–8).

REFLECT AND ACT: How does Christian nationalism distort the teachings of Jesus? How can you re-center the core teachings of Christianity—that all are created in the image of God and that we show love for God by loving our neighbor—in your life? How has white supremacy impacted your faith tradition and your theology? Share your reflections with a person or group, and listen to their responses.

THREE

Step Three

Denounce Violence

In August 2017, I was sitting in the kitchen of my in-laws' home in Texas, watching the horrifying events of the Unite the Right rally unfold in Charlottesville, Virginia. I sat with my Jewish family as white supremacists and self-proclaimed neo-Nazis chanted, "Jews will not replace us!" and marched through the streets with tiki torches. Not far from the University of Virginia—founded by Thomas Jefferson, one of the architects of religious freedom law in the United States—paramilitary and militia groups descended en masse. Men wearing tactical gear and carrying weapons suddenly appeared to be occupying this college town.

In the end, a man who promoted white supremacist views drove his car into a crowd, killing one person—Heather

Heyer, age thirty-two—and injuring dozens more. Two Virginia State Police troopers—Lt. H. Jay Cullen, forty-eight, and Berke M. M. Bates, forty—were killed when their helicopter crashed while they were surveilling the violent demonstrations.

I experienced a range of emotions in those first days after the violence: shock, disgust, deep grief, disorientation, anger, despair, resolve. I was moved by a firsthand account written by Alan Zimmerman, president of Congregation Beth Israel in Charlottesville, on the impact of the intimidation on one faith community. He shared how three men in fatigues carrying rifles stood across the street from his house of worship while they held a service inside. "Several times, parades of Nazis passed our building, shouting, 'There's the synagogue!' followed by chants of 'Sieg Heil.' . . . Some carried flags with swastikas and other Nazi symbols," he wrote. "When services ended, my heart broke as I advised congregants that it would be safer to leave the temple through the back entrance rather than through the front, and to please go in groups."

When a community is scared to gather for worship and prayer because of intimidation and threats of violence, their religious freedom has been violated. What felt most alarming was the normalization of terror, hate, and violence that were perpetuated by President Trump's comments that there were "very fine people, on both sides." I knew then that all of us had to play a role in defending freedom and diversity from hate groups.

About a year later came the murders at Tree of Life synagogue in Pittsburgh, the deadliest attack on Jews in US history. On Saturday morning, October 27, 2018, in Pittsburgh's Squirrel Hill neighborhood—one of the largest Jewish neighborhoods in the United States—about seventy-five people from three separate Jewish congregations that shared the Tree of Life synagogue space had gathered inside the building for various religious services. A middle-aged man, armed with an AR-15 and several Glock handguns, entered the house of worship shouting antisemitic slurs. He began shooting.

By the end of his rampage, eleven people were dead, and several more were wounded. Those murdered in the Tree of Life attack were Joyce Fienberg, Richard Gottfried, Rose Mallinger, Dr. Jerry Rabinowitz, brothers Cecil Rosenthal and David Rosenthal, Bernice Simon and her husband, Sylvan Simon, Daniel Stein, Melvin Wax, and Irving Younger. The oldest victim was ninety-seven years old.

The gunman, Robert D. Bowers, had an extensive history of espousing antisemitic, white supremacist, racist, and Christian nationalist views on social media. In the days leading up to the Tree of Life attack, Bowers posted a menacing message on the social media platform Gab and included a link to the Hebrew Immigrant Aid Society (HIAS), an organization that helps vulnerable migrants around the world find safe harbor and that was hosting Shabbat services for refugees at synagogues throughout the nation. Dor Hadash, one of the three congregations that shared the Tree of Life space, hosted an HIAS Shabbat a week before the attack. A few hours before he walked into the synagogue and murdered eleven people, Bowers posted a message on Gab saying, "HIAS likes to bring invaders in that kill our people. I can't sit by and watch my people get slaughtered. Screw your optics, I'm going in."

Gab, which was created in 2016 as a so-called free speech site, had become a haven for extremists for hateful conspiracy theories. Bowers's profile description on Gab, which the site removed after the synagogue massacre, incorporated visual references to Nazism and read, "Jews are the children of Satan."

On June 16, 2023, a jury found Bowers guilty on all sixty-three federal charges, including eleven counts of obstructing the free exercise of religious beliefs resulting in death. "I am grateful to God for getting us to this day," Tree of Life Rabbi Jeffrey Myers, who survived the attack, said in a written statement after the verdict. "And I am thankful for the law enforcement who ran into danger to rescue me, and the US Attorney who stood up in court to defend my right to pray."

The deadliest synagogue attack in our nation's history did not happen in a vacuum. The murders took place eleven days before the 2018 midterm elections. For months, midterm campaigns had been filled with bitterness and vitriol. Some right-wing candidates had stoked the racist and antisemitic rhetoric, aiming it at their opponents and employing it to terrify the electorate. In the week leading up to the Tree of Life murders, the country saw a series of pipe bombs targeting a range of prominent Democrats and groups considered supporters of the party, including former President Barack Obama, former US Secretary of State Hillary Rodham Clinton, philanthropist George Soros, and CNN.

Five months after the Tree of Life massacre, a white supremacist murdered fifty-one people in two mosques in Christchurch, New Zealand. A month later, a nineteen-year-old white man walked into the Chabad of Poway Jewish community near San Diego, murdered one woman, and shot three others, including a rabbi. Before his attack on the morning of the last day of Passover, the shooter, John T. Earnest, posted an online screed citing inspiration from both the Christchurch and Tree of Life shootings. We see some of these perpetrators spout similar ideologies, such as the great replacement theory that white people are being "replaced" by Jewish people, immigrants, and racial minorities, in their reasoning for violence.

I recount all these horrors to make a critical point: we should not assume these shootings are isolated or localized incidents. If we ignore the connections between these events—the root structure of hatred and bigotry that links the shooters and the networks and the theories—we fail to see the reality that is confronting us. Thinking that any of these were isolated incidents or downplaying them as the result of a lone-wolf shooter is not just downright wrong; it's dangerous as it allows us to turn away from the peril we face.

One of the important tasks of our work is to denounce violence and threats of violence wherever we see them. Rejecting violence and pursuing peace is an esteemed part of the Christian tradition, with analogues in other major religions as well. We can find the source and sustenance for our work against violence in our faith.

When I use the term *violence* in this step, I am referring primarily to physical violence, that is, the use of physical force to cause injury, harm, pain, or damage to any person or property. I also include threats of physical violence, which are words or actions that cause injury, harm, pain, or damage to any person or property. In other parts of this book, I talk about the psychological violence of Christian nationalism, the resulting intergenerational trauma, and how certain policies can be violent manifestations of Christian nationalism that can injure, harm, and damage people and their communities.

LIVING FAITHFULLY IN A VIOLENT WORLD

One of Christian nationalism's most blatant distortions of the gospel of Jesus is its embrace of violence and use of scripture to justify violent means. Jesus's persistent teachings and life example were ones of nonviolence. I believe that Jesus, whose teachings included "Blessed are the peacemakers, for they will be called children of God" (Matt. 5:9 NRSVUE), would be horrified to see his image and name used to justify violence in any instance.

Given the words and example of Christ, we can be confident in our denunciation of violence. Our culture is undeniably a violent one, and we live in a violent world. But as followers of Christ, we are instructed to love our enemies and to turn the other cheek—to respond to violence with nonviolence and love.

Creating long-lasting, justice-filled peace will always be difficult, and we might be tempted to minimize the denunciation of violence as somehow easy or simplistic. But that doesn't mean we should stop denouncing violence. We are living in a moment in history in which it is imperative to stand against all forms of violence: gun violence, political violence, rhetorical violence, and hate crimes. These types of violence are not discrete categories but often overlapping. They are also all connected in direct and indirect ways to Christian nationalism, as we will now consider.

GUN VIOLENCE

One marker of the violence that surrounds us is American society's idolatrous devotion to guns and gun culture. It is killing us. And there is a tangible connection between gun culture and Christian nationalism.

According to survey data, adherence to Christian nationalist beliefs is strongly correlated with opposition to gun control. A common refrain heard in the wake of the seemingly incessant mass shootings in the United States is the need to "protect our God-given Second Amendment right" to bear arms.

As in many other areas of law and policy that are driven in part by Christian nationalism, racism is also at play when it comes to opposition to gun control or expansion of gun rights, including the proliferation of open-carry laws. Political scientists have drawn connections between the carrying of guns as a form of intimidation and the defense of "white democracy." Even when it isn't explicitly stated, we should remember that using the language of Christian nationalism also often includes the unstated but very present context of racism and white supremacy.

After the murder of nineteen schoolchildren and two teachers at Robb Elementary School in Uvalde, Texas—which was merely ten days after ten people were murdered in the Buffalo mass shooting—Congressman Brian Babin (R-Texas) proclaimed, "The United States of America has always had guns. It's our history. We were built on the Judeo-Christian foundation and with guns." Repeating such hollow rhetoric that ties God and country like this only exacerbates the scourge of gun violence. We face the slaughter of innocents in the United States unlike any other nation on earth does. Instead of trying to justify it, Christians need to begin denouncing it.

POLITICAL VIOLENCE

The growing approval of politically motivated violence among Americans is deeply concerning. In the 2023 American Values Survey, PRRI asked respondents if they agreed with this statement: "Because things have gotten so far off track, true American patriots may have to resort to violence in order to save our country." Nearly a quarter of respondents (23 percent) agreed with the potential need to take up arms to "save our country." It was the first time that support for political violence peaked above 20 percent since researchers began asking the question in 2021.

The January 6, 2021, insurrection provides a stark example of how Christian nationalism can be used to galvanize groups of people to disregard the democratic process and engage in political violence. In 2022, the organization I lead, BJC, worked with the Freedom From Religion Foundation to produce a comprehensive report on the ways that Christian nationalism influenced the January 6 attack. The report argues that understanding the violence of January 6 requires paying attention to the events that led up to it.

In the time leading up to January 6, religious leaders were using the language of spiritual warfare to call people into the cause. They organized events in Washington, DC, such as the Million MAGA March on November 14, 2020, and the Jericho March's "Let the Church ROAR" rally on December 12, 2020—both of which ended in violence. After the December 12 event, four Black churches were vandalized, and a Black Lives Matter banner was destroyed outside of another in Washington. Andrew Seidel, a coeditor of and contributor to the report, describes these marches as "dry runs" and "typical of terrorist attacks." Seidel offers many examples, including this recounting of a speech at the December 12 Jericho March event:

> The Rev. Kevin Jessip made the Christian nationalism explicit. "Some have said this is not a Christian nation. I'm telling you this is a Judeo-Christian nation. . . . Today, I call this the warrior mandate, a battle cry, a call to arms." And then, almost as an afterthought, he qualified the belligerence with "in the spiritual realm." He explained that the "battle cry" is a "mobilization of God's men made holy by the blood of Jesus Christ and empowered by the gift of the baptism of the Holy Spirit. This battle cry is a Christian call to all Christian men . . . as we prepare for a strategic gathering of men in this hour to dispel the Kingdom of Darkness."

The violence of January 6, 2021, is better known than the violence of these lead-up events. In the days immediately after January 6, many political and religious leaders, including members of Trump's Republican Party, condemned the violence. But as time went on, the violent rhetoric crept back into their speeches. While speaking at a Christian college in Michigan in February 2022, for example, Florida governor Ron DeSantis twisted scripture into a thinly veiled call to arms. In the wake of the attack on the US Capitol, we can only consider language such as this to be rhetorical recklessness: "Put on the full armor of God. Stand firm against the Left's schemes," Gov. DeSantis told the audience at Hillsdale

College. "You will face flaming arrows, but if you have the shield of faith, you will overcome them, and in Florida we walk the line here. And I can tell you this, I have only begun to fight."

Gov. DeSantis's words lead us to another kind of violence: rhetorical violence. Leaders whose messages are steeped in violent rhetoric can try to deny the connections between their words and the actions of others. But those claims ring hollow when we look at the many ways their followers take violence out of the metaphorical realm and make it real.

RHETORICAL VIOLENCE

ReAwaken America is part political rally, part religious revival, part circus sideshow for conspiracy theories and election denialism. The traveling event was cofounded in 2021 by Clay Clark, a business owner from Tulsa who sued the city of Tulsa over its mask mandate (he dropped the lawsuit five months later). Clark's cofounder is a retired US Army Lieutenant General who briefly served as Trump's national security adviser, Michael Flynn. This event often features Trump insiders, including some of the evangelical Christian pastors who have been his vocal supporters for nearly a decade.

My colleagues and I had been tracking the ReAwaken phenomenon since its launch in November 2021. Flynn said something around that time that caught my attention: "If we are going to have one nation under God, which we must, we have to have one religion. One nation under God and one religion under God." That message remains consistent at the ReAwaken events, which are unapologetically full of Christian nationalism in message, flavor, and goals.

I had watched the ReAwaken America tour from a distance, horrified by the accounts I read. It was easy for me to dismiss the events and the attendees as extreme, but I decided I needed to see what exactly was happening in those spaces. So a BJC colleague and I got tickets for the two-day event at Trump's Miami resort in May 2023.

When we walked into the hotel event room for the Pastors for Trump pre-event, the shoulder-to-shoulder crowd of about 400 people was singing a praise and worship song. Many attendees seemed moved by the song, closing their eyes and raising their arms aloft. Some people were so overcome with emotion that they cried. Nothing about the worship song was overtly political; you might hear this song at any nondenominational church anywhere in the United States, and it was clearly familiar to many of those present. Once the praise and worship was done, there were rally-type speeches and calls for donations. Flynn delivered a long speech, followed by other speakers who proclaimed "prophecies" about Trump being reelected. Roger Stone, a convicted felon and one of Trump's political operatives, spoke at the event, as did at least three pastors from Oklahoma.

One of those Oklahoma pastors, John Bennett, made a speech that included some very explicit calls for political violence. As he exhorted the crowd, they responded with hoots and hollers, fist pumps, and choruses of "Amen" and "Yes, Lord!" "We're at a time and place where evil is called good and good is called evil," Bennett said from the podium:

> We're at a time and place where God is rising up an army of faithful believers. And make no mistake about it, we are here for such a time as this, and I'm excited about that, and so should you—Did you ever hear that Christian song, it goes something to the effect of, "Lord, my enemies have me surrounded, but you have my enemies surrounded"? That's where we're at today. You know what, in military terms, as General Flynn can understand, we had a famous military general one time, he said one of his Marines came up to him and said, "Sir, we're surrounded." And he said, "That simplifies things; now we can shoot in every direction."

"You should be proud to be in God's army," Bennett continued as the crowd cheered. "We are God's army, and God is raising up some Davids, some Daniels, some Moseses, and some Elijahs for such a time as this. We need more Elijahs on Mount Carmel that [bring] down the Holy Ghost Spirit of fire down upon the enemies that we face today, because we can, and we will win this fight in the name of Jesus."

At this, the crowd went wild. Looking around me at the fervent and feverish crowd, I thought it seemed like they were answering a spiritual call—what this pastor was asking them to do. And I felt for them. I understand the kind of emotional impact a meaningful religious service can deliver, and I also felt sadness at the hollowness of this particular gathering, which was directed solely at spreading misinformation and stoking violence in an effort to secure power for a political candidate.

People sometimes ask me how much of the Christian nationalism movement is genuinely a religious cause and how much is purely political. I often say it is a political cause that uses religious language to pursue its aims. I still think that's true, at least for the leaders and conveners of events like ReAwaken America. But watching the people in the crowd that day, I saw firsthand the way that Christian nationalism can feel like a religious experience as well. We will explore the use of baptisms at the ReAwaken America tour in step 5. I saw the emotional and spiritual dimensions of the movement, the way that ecstasy and worship and fervor combined to create a religious experience.

Yet what is that religion? For those in attendance, it appears that so much of their spiritual calling has become this political calling, which they believe is a religious cause. When Bennett was calling for an army to rise—and, basically, for them to start shooting at the enemies that have them surrounded—people in the crowd lifted their hands in a posture of prayer and praise, some saying, "Thank you, Jesus," and "I'm here for you, Jesus." It's clear they genuinely believe this is what they're meant to be doing.

Much of this spiritual warfare language is extreme, yes. We'd like to believe it's a vocabulary on the fringes. But it's important to understand what's happening in explicitly Christian nationalist spaces. We need to know the kind of language that's being used. We need to understand how effective Christian nationalist organizing has become, how it is galvanizing people around the cause of—essentially—creating a white Christian America for white Christian Americans.

WHAT HISTORICAL VIOLENCE SHOWS US

History teaches us the dire results of turning Christian witness into cheerleading for an authoritarian leader. Tragically—both for untold numbers of people who have been killed and oppressed and for Christianity itself—white Christian nationalism has caused Christians to minimize or abandon tenets of their faith to align themselves with political power.

One glaring example of Christian complicity with violent power is the rise of Nazism in Germany, where the vast majority of the population was Protestant or Catholic Christian in the 1930s. Rev. John Matthews, a Lutheran minister and expert on the life and work of Dietrich Bonhoeffer, urges people to decipher parallels between our moment in history and that one. In a webinar organized by World Without Genocide in January 2023, Rev. Matthews described how Hitler fused nationalism, authoritarianism, and a corrupted version of Christianity, which gave a certain legitimacy to his delusions about racial, moral, and global supremacy: "This dangerous phenomenon . . . has reared its ugly head in the United States more dramatically in the last few years. But do we recognize that?"

The extreme Nazi policies that many Germans dismissed as so much saber-rattling before Hitler came to power manifested, only a few years later, as the Holocaust. Rev. Matthews pointed out that authoritarian leaders who use intimidation and violence to achieve power will use it in order to stay in power too. "Once the state has the unconditional endorsement of the religious establishment, nothing is off limits. Anything is acceptable because we know the phrase 'God is on our side.'"

It's a pattern that has been and continues to be repeated throughout history. Apartheid in South Africa. Hindu nationalism in India. The genocide of Rohingya Muslims in majority-Buddhist Myanmar. The Russian Orthodox Church's consecration of Vladimir Putin's invasion of Ukraine. The concurrent rise of Christian nationalism in Viktor Orbán's Hungary.

When humans in power believe God is on their side, doors open to chilling scenarios. No, we shouldn't prognosticate irresponsibly or suggest we're doomed to repeat the past. But we should carefully examine times in history when religion has supported state-sanctioned violence, and we should learn the lessons embedded there. Religion should never be used to justify violence, and when we see that happening, we must denounce it.

INTERFAITH RESPONSES TO
ANTI-MUSLIM VIOLENCE

The violence that Christian nationalism inspires is often directed at religious groups other than Christians. Christian nationalism is an ideology that feeds and intensifies other forms of discrimination, including Islamophobia, antisemitism, anti-Sikh sentiment, and violence against religious minorities in the United States. Racism is almost always also at play in these hate crimes because of the ways religion has been racialized.

Research has shown that the more closely people adhere to Christian nationalism, the more likely they are to fear and distrust Muslims, hold anti-immigrant views, and fear refugees. In *Taking America Back for God: Christian Nationalism in the United States*, Dr. Perry and Dr. Whitehead find a direct correlation between Christian nationalism beliefs and agreement with the statement "Refugees from the Middle East pose a terrorist threat to the United States." It was precisely this sentiment that inspired the campaign promise that Trump made good on, after his 2016 election, in his administration's infamous Muslim travel ban.

While Muslims are not a monolith—ethnically or even theologically—they often are treated as a singular and suspect population that harbors inherently violent impulses and deserves discrimination. "It's a form of racism that is based both on skin color and assumed cultural and religious attributes," according to Dr. Todd Green, a former adviser on Islamophobia in Europe with the US State Department.

In the 2016 presidential election, white evangelicals voted in droves (81 percent) for Donald Trump, who said during his campaign, "I think Islam hates us." Evangelical support for Trump later translated into solid support for his Muslim travel ban—three-quarters of white evangelicals expressed support for the move just a month after Trump took office. White evangelicals continue to harbor negative opinions of Muslims at much higher levels (44 percent) compared with people in most other faith communities, according to a 2019 poll by the Institute for Social Policy and Understanding.

"What we have been witnessing for quite some time is the instrumentalization of and support for racial and religious bigotry by many white evangelicals in an effort to embrace and defend a white Christian America," wrote Dr. Green. "White evangelical support for discriminatory policies and practices that have targeted Muslims—detentions, deportations, extraordinary renditions, torture, surveillance, profiling, the Muslim ban—must be understood as both an extension and a manifestation of this white Christian nationalist project."

At BJC, one of our closest allies in combating Christian nationalism is the Shoulder to Shoulder Campaign, a multifaith coalition of religious denominations and faith-based organizations committed to building a society where all are treated with dignity and respect. The campaign mobilizes faith communities in the United States as strategic partners in countering, addressing, and preventing anti-Muslim discrimination and violence.

Shoulder to Shoulder was founded during a surge in anti-Muslim rhetoric and hatred in the United States, when leaders of several religious communities and faith-based organizations approached the Islamic Society of North America to ask how they could help the Muslim community during the crisis. The plan to build an Islamic center a few hundred yards from the site of the attacks of September 11, 2001, in lower Manhattan was spurring controversy.

On September 7, 2010, more than forty religious leaders from Christian, Jewish, and Muslim communities—including the US Conference of Catholic Bishops, Union of Reform Judaism, the Evangelical Lutheran Church in America, The Episcopal Church, the Progressive National Baptist Convention, the National Council of Churches, American Baptist Churches USA, and many others—came together to issue a statement expressing their commitment to work against anti-Muslim discrimination and toward the ideals of religious freedom and pluralism on which the United States is founded. The statement read, in part, "We are convinced that spiritual leaders representing the various faiths in the United States have a moral responsibility to stand together and to denounce categorically derision, misinformation or outright bigotry directed against any religious group in this country. Silence is not an option. Only by taking this stand, can spiritual leaders fulfill the highest calling of our respective faiths, and thereby help to create a safer and stronger America for all of our people."

Since its founding, Shoulder to Shoulder has continued that mission and expanded its reach. The coalition has mustered support and organized responses when anti-Muslim sentiments have spiked in the United States—for example, during the COVID-19 pandemic as xenophobic narratives increased, Nina Fernando, the executive director of Shoulder to Shoulder, told me. "This is not just a Muslim issue," said Fernando, who is not Muslim. "This is an issue we all need to work on, which is why we're working toward having faith allies take ownership of the issue and do the work within their own communities."

Anti-Muslim bigotry affects not only Muslims but also those who are *perceived* to be Muslim, including "the Sikh community, Hindus, Buddhists—really any Black and brown communities," Fernando said. She recalled the murder of Balbir Singh Sodhi, a fifty-two-year-old Sikh man who was fatally shot at the gas station he owned in Mesa, Arizona, on September 15, 2001, by a gunman who believed him to be a Muslim. The gunman, Frank Silva Roque, reportedly said after the 9/11 attacks he was "going to go out and shoot some towel heads," and later he opened fire on Sodhi, who was with a landscaper planting flowers on the gas station property. Later that same day, Roque shot at a Lebanese American clerk but missed. He then drove his truck to his former residence, which had been purchased by a local Afghani family, and fired multiple rounds at the house.

In many ways, Shoulder to Shoulder's mission mirrors that of Christians Against Christian Nationalism. Combating

Christian nationalism is why Shoulder to Shoulder exists, Fernando said: "At its best, it is a solidarity effort that is meant to work alongside those who are directly affected by the issue, but it is also to bring those who are not necessarily directly affected [by anti-Muslim sentiments] into the work as well. When we do the deeper analysis, when we think about our faith values, all of us are affected by this issue—it's about all of us in an interconnected, pluralistic society coming together to address and end white Christian nationalism."

One of the most effective ways Shoulder to Shoulder has found to combat Christian nationalism and anti-Muslim rhetoric is by fostering personal relationships between Muslims and non-Muslims—often by connecting them around a dinner table. Every Ramadan, the campaign coordinates a nationwide list of interfaith iftars, the traditional meal eaten after sunset during each of the forty days of Ramadan to break the fast. "In 2019, we went on a Ramadan road trip and visited many of those iftars," Fernando recalled. "Some of them were sponsored by the city and were in convention centers, some were in people's homes, some in parks. The one in Atlanta was just gorgeous, right in the middle of the city, showing how—quite literally—sharing a meal with your Muslim neighbors, getting to know them, taking part in their traditions helped to make connections between people."

Shoulder to Shoulder provides programming for communities large and small across the United States. Local religious or civic groups in communities with hate-group activity often invite residents to come to an educational or training program. One such recent experience in Minnesota left an indelible impression on Fernando: "We were preparing to go to Willmar, Minnesota, which was making national news at the time because of growing hate-group activity in the region." She continued:

> The only flight available for me was in the evening, and I was going to be traveling alone. . . . I am a brown woman, and from what I was reading in the news, I was not welcome there. I was scared. But when I arrived and walked into the community center to meet the interfaith group that asked us to host the training session, I was blown away by the welcome we received. The folks, who were from various backgrounds, were eager to have the training. Not only did our training attract Christians in the community who said, "We need training because we need to tell our stories"; it also brought in other minority communities who had been "invisibilized," if you will: who lived in the area but kept to themselves. They felt like it was a safe place to connect with other people and push back against the groups that were promoting hate.

Denouncing violence, combating anti-Muslim sentiment, countering any other kind of white supremacist or xenophobic rhetoric: these tasks don't always have to involve a grand gesture, she said. "All of us have a role to play, whether that may be having lunch with a neighbor, advocating for policy changes on Capitol Hill, and everything in between. You don't have to be an expert to recognize the humanity of another person. You don't have to know all the facts about Islam to recognize the humanity of someone who is Muslim."

READ: "But I say to you who are willing to hear: Love your enemies. Do good to those who hate you. Bless those who curse you. Pray for those who mistreat you. If someone slaps you on the cheek, offer the other one as well" (Luke 6:27–29).

REFLECT AND ACT: Pay attention to how Christian language and scripture are being used to justify violence. Denounce violent *rhetoric* as much as you would denounce violent action itself.

FOUR

Step Four

Commit to the Separation of Church and State

Representative Lauren Boebert was tired of the separation of church and state. Addressing Sunday-morning worshippers in a Colorado church on June 26, 2022, Rep. Boebert, a Republican from Colorado, explained why. "The reason we had so many overreaching regulations in our nation is because the church complied," she said. She paused for effect and then enunciated each word of her next two sentences slowly, deliberately, and with precision: "The church is supposed to direct the government. The government is not supposed to direct the church. That is not how our founding fathers intended it. And I'm tired of this separation of church and state junk that's not in the Constitution. It was in a stinking letter, and it means nothing like what they say it does." A chorus of amens filled the air.

Two weeks earlier, at a Christian center in Colorado Springs, Rep. Boebert told the audience, "I want to let y'all know, right now is the time for the church to influence the nation. . . . This is the vision that our founding fathers had from the very beginning."

Rep. Boebert's comments, while colorful and likely meant to elicit media coverage and campaign donations—and they did—reflect a deep misunderstanding of the Constitution. They mischaracterize the way American law protects religious freedom through the institutional separation of church and state. These untruths have circulated for decades, and Boebert is not alone in her views. Shortly after being elected Speaker of the House in fall 2023, Rep. Mike Johnson, a Republican from Louisiana, told a reporter, "The separation of church and state is a misnomer. People misunderstand it. Of course, it comes from a phrase that was in a letter that Jefferson wrote. It's not in the Constitution. And what he was explaining is they did not want the government to encroach upon the church—not that they didn't want principles of faith to have influence on our public life. It's exactly the opposite."

These comments from Speaker Johnson and Rep. Boebert depart from a long-standing consensus among people of both major political parties that the principle of the separation of church and state, far from being "junk," is essential to freedom and equality. Ending Christian nationalism

requires understanding and promoting the proper relationship between religion and government—one that fosters
religious freedom for all people, protects the independence of
religious institutions, and is supported by the Constitution.

Given the amount of misinformation out there—including
untruths spread by high-ranking officials—some myth-
busting is in order.

"AN AMERICAN ORIGINAL"

Rep. Boebert, Speaker Johnson, and others who claim the
exact phrase "separation of church and state" is not in the
Constitution are technically correct. But the concept is
inscribed throughout the entire document. The phrases
"separation of powers" and "checks and balances" are not
in the Constitution either. Yet it is widely accepted that the
framers of Articles I, II, and III of the founding document set
up a democratic system of government in which power would
remain with the people by ensuring that no one branch of
government would hold too much control over the whole. As
my predecessor at BJC, Brent Walker, says, "The Constitution
may not have those words—church-state separation—in it,
but those who wrote the Constitution and other early observ-
ers had the words in *them*."

"Separation of church and state" is shorthand for the way
the founders envisioned the independence of the institutions
of religion and government. Far from creating a government
that would be controlled by religion, the wise and imperfect

framers of the Constitution in 1787 set up a system that would favor no group among religions. The Constitution is a secular, not a religious, charter. Christianity is not mentioned at all in the founding document. Neither is God. The only time that "religion" or "religious" is mentioned in the original Constitution is in Article VI, which provides, "The Senators and Representatives before mentioned, and the Members of the several State Legislatures, and all executive and judicial Officers, both of the United States and of the several States, shall be bound by Oath or Affirmation, to support this Constitution; *but no religious Test shall ever be required as a Qualification to any Office or public Trust under the United States*" (italics added).

The right to represent American citizens as an elected official is not based on one's religion—or lack thereof. In establishing this rule, the framers provided there would be no favored group among religions. When responding to claims that the founders intended the country to be a Christian nation, I find that the single most effective response is to point people back to the Constitution and to this particular provision. Reminding friends and acquaintances of the secular nature of the document and the way it remains neutral with regard to religion helps dispel the Christian nation myth, particularly with regard to the legal structure of the country.

As for the metaphor of the "wall of separation between church and state," Rep. Boebert and Speaker Johnson are both right that Thomas Jefferson used that language in a

letter written in 1802 to a group of Baptist ministers in Con-
necticut, organized as the Danbury Baptist Association. The
Baptists had written to Jefferson to congratulate him on
his election and to encourage him to protect religious freedom as an inalienable right. Jefferson famously responded,
"Believing with you that religion is a matter which lies solely
between Man & his God, that he owes account to none other
for his faith or his worship, that the legitimate powers of government reach actions only, & not opinions, I contemplate
with sovereign reverence that act of the whole American
people which declared that their legislature should 'make no
law respecting an establishment of religion, or prohibiting
the free exercise thereof,' thus building a wall of separation
between Church & State."

Others during the founding period supported the concept
of separation of church and state as well. James Madison,
the fourth president of the United States and called by some
the "father of the Constitution," wrote in 1819, "The number,
the industry, and the morality of the priesthood and the devotion
of the people have been manifestly increased by the total separation of the Church from the State." Alexis de Tocqueville also
used the phrase in *Democracy in America*. Having spent ten
months during 1831 and 1832 traveling through the United
States, the French diplomat and political theorist wrote, "In
France, I had almost always seen the spirit of religion and
the spirit of freedom marching in opposite directions. But in
America I found they were intimately united and that they
reigned in common over the same country . . . [T]hey all

attributed the peaceful dominion of religion in their country mainly to the separation of church and state.... I did not meet a single individual, of the clergy or the laity, who was not of the same opinion on this point."

The fact that Tocqueville included separation of church and state in his study of American politics speaks to the importance it held at the founding period and to the way outsiders viewed the new country and its political makeup. Andrew Seidel, constitutional lawyer and author of *The Founding Myth: Why Christian Nationalism Is Un-American*, told me he thinks Americans can feel pride about the wall of separation between church and state, which is "an American original. It's an American invention. The idea was floating around in the Enlightenment, but it was first implemented in the American experiment. In the history of the world, in the history of humanity, up to that point, no other nation or people had sought to protect the ability of their citizens to think freely by separating religion and government. I think we really ought to be proud of that fact, and we shouldn't let people undermine it with myths of a 'Christian nation founding.'"

Suggesting that "the church is supposed to direct the government," as Rep. Boebert claims, imperils a core aspect of our democratic commitments. "Our Constitution was the first to declare that power comes from people, not gods. The words 'We the People' are poetic, but there is so much more," Seidel told me. "There's a whole lot wrong with the Constitution, especially as originally written. But those secular foundations really did make it unique. They're genuine contributions, not just to political science and thought but to humanity."

FREEDOM OR TOLERANCE?

So why is the separation of church and state so essential to the protection of religious freedom? It is first important to understand the difference between religious *freedom* and religious *tolerance*. The terms are often used interchangeably, but there is a big difference between the two.

Religious *freedom* (also sometimes referred to as religious liberty) in a political or legal sense means that one can choose to believe (or not) and then practice, exercise, or otherwise act on that belief without unnecessary interference from the government. Notice that while freedom of *belief* is unlimited, freedom of *action* is not. In any society, our freedoms are interconnected with the freedoms of others. If our right of exercise were unlimited, we would constantly infringe on the freedom of others. When disputes arise, the government—in the legal system, the court—acts as the arbiter between competing freedoms. In doing so, it should maintain neutrality when it comes to religion, not advancing or prohibiting any one religion over another nor the practice of religion over the freedom not to practice religion.

Inherent in the idea of religious *tolerance* is power. In this view, the government has chosen a preferred religion, and all other religions are merely tolerated but not accepted as equal. If I merely tolerate you, then I retain the power to *not* tolerate you.

People in the founding generation understood the difference between religious freedom and religious toleration. Virginia Baptist leader John Leland, a contemporary and neighbor of James Madison in Virginia, called tolerance "despicable." In the *Virginia Chronicle* in 1790, Leland wrote, "The notion of a Christian commonwealth should be exploded forever.... Government should protect every man in thinking and speaking freely, and see that one does not abuse another. The liberty I contend for is more than toleration. The very idea of toleration is despicable; it supposes that some have a preeminence above the rest to grant indulgence; whereas all should be equally free, Jews, Turks [Muslims], Pagans and Christians."

President George Washington also spoke about the importance of liberty over tolerance. In his letter to the Touro Synagogue in 1790, Washington wrote:

The Citizens of the United States of America have a right to applaud themselves for having given to mankind examples of an enlarged and liberal policy—a policy worthy of imitation. All possess alike liberty of conscience and immunities of citizenship. It is now no more that toleration is spoken of as if it were the indulgence of one class of people that another enjoyed the exercise of their inherent natural rights, for, happily, the Government of the United States, which gives to bigotry no sanction, to persecution no assistance, requires only that they who live under its protection should demean themselves as good citizens in giving it on all occasions their effectual support.

Now we must note the ugly truth here: though the prose is beautiful, Washington and the other founders violated this ideal from the very beginning. Citizenship was granted only to white persons from the very beginning, including in the Naturalization Act of 1790. The vast majority of citizens at the time claimed a Protestant identity. Race-based slavery and the theft of lands and genocide of Indigenous populations are all despicable, violent practices that have caused massive intergenerational harm and trauma with which this country still has not fully reckoned. Understanding the full context of history is crucial if we are not to keep making the same horrific mistakes today.

Given this history, the Constitution is best read as a statement of principles rather than as a description of the political society that the framers created. But the principle stated is one that protects the institutional separation of church and state. The faulty interpretation of constitutional law that Rep. Boebert, Speaker Johnson, and others peddle is not one that protects the full flourishing of religious freedom. Rather, Christian nationalism promotes Christian privilege in law, politics, and society and, at best, *toleration* of other faiths and the nonreligious. The ideal of equality regardless of religion is discarded in favor of an effective caste system, with only white Christians as full citizens and everyone else having effective second-class citizenship.

This exclusionary and divisive system is perpetuated by the myth that the United States was founded as, is now, and always should be a Christian nation. As we saw in step 1, this glorified and fictional account of our history sanctifies the founders and sacralizes our founding documents. The myth transforms political actors into God's agents on earth, carrying out a divine plan for American leadership and dominance in the world.

Religious freedom is the aim; religious tolerance remains merely a pale shadow of it. And here's the thing our neighbors and family members convinced by Christian nationalism need to remember: preserving religious freedom is important not only for historically marginalized groups. Separation of church and state is also an important protection for those who practice the majority religion. While it's difficult to convince some people of this fact, it's a critical truth to which we now turn: that is, in striving to "protect" Christianity by knocking down the wall between church and state, Christians end up harming the faith they claim to hold so dear.

WHEN THE CHURCH BECOMES A TOOL OF THE STATE

Those who push a Christian nation mythology and seek to legislate Christian nationalism into law, policy, and political practice seem to be working with dual assumptions: that government support of Christianity helps it flourish and that government neutrality when it comes to religion would hurt Christianity. But data contradicts both these arguments.

A study published in 2022 by the journal *Politics and Religion* gauged the impact of various forms of religious favoritism by the state on the religiosity of its citizens. The results of the study, which spanned 174 countries and multiple decades, found that state support for one religion or religious institution over all others with the goal of strengthening the faith had the *opposite* effect. "Religious institutions that receive favorable treatment from the state lose ground relative to those that do not," wrote the study's author, Dr. Dan Koev. He continued:

In states with an established and preferentially funded religion, the dominant religion of the state declined as a share of population by 3.4 percent on average in the period 1990–2010. In contrast, in states without such religious favoritism, the share of the population belonging to the most popular religion grew by 13 percent. In states with an official and preferentially funded religion, minority religions performed substantially better than the established one . . . [O]n average, enjoying an official status and special access to state resources [had a negative impact on] the growth of a religion, both as a share of total population and relative to other religions in the state. . . . Overall, these findings suggest that, when it comes to religious affiliation, official state recognition and state funding may harm institutions [they are] meant to support and protect.

In other words, the study confirms what many proponents of religious liberty have known for centuries: official favoritism of a religion by the nation-state actually harms that religion. It jeopardizes the soul freedom that is essential to expression of faith. Religion must be voluntary to be vital and unfettered by the state to be truly free.

Again, Baptist pastor John Leland wrote wisely on this topic way back in the early part of the nineteenth century: "Experience, the best teacher, has informed us that the fondness of magistrates to foster Christianity has done it more harm than all the persecutions ever did. Persecution, like a lion, tears the saints to death, but leaves Christianity pure: state establishment of religion, like a bear, hugs the saints, but corrupts Christianity, and reduces it to a level with state policy."

More than 150 years later, another Baptist pastor, Rev. Dr. Martin Luther King Jr., also affirmed that the separation of church and state is the best arrangement for religious institutions. "The church must be reminded that it is not the master or the servant of the state, but rather the conscience of the state," Dr. King said. "It must be the guide and the critic of the state, and never its tool. If the church does not recapture its prophetic zeal, it will become an irrelevant social club without moral or spiritual authority."

Dr. King's words are both truthful and prescient. The decline of the impact of religious institutions has coincided with the growing incursions on church-state separation over the past few decades, from both sides of that proverbial wall. Some in governmental leadership have reacted to the waning influence of religion in society by trying to prop up religion in ways that will inevitably harm its independence and vitality; meanwhile, those in religious leadership have simultaneously sought political power, to the detriment of their prophetic voice. History is an important guide, however. Between the eighteenth century and the twentieth century, Baptists grew from a fringe, persecuted sect in many areas of the country to the largest Protestant group in the United States, due in large part to the *dis*establishment of religion in the founding period. A similar phenomenon helped other Protestant denominations flourish during the same period.

But there is evidence that the framers also had in mind growing diversity beyond the sects that were known at the time. In 1787, the Federal Farmer wrote, "It is true, we are not disposed to differ much, at present, about religion; but when we are making a constitution, it is to be hoped, for ages and millions yet unborn, why not establish the free exercise of religion, as a part of the national compact." We turn now to the importance of separation of the institutions of religion and government for everyone, including those who practice faiths other than Christianity or who do not claim a religious identity or tradition.

PROTECTING RELIGIOUS FREEDOM IN A PLURALISTIC SOCIETY

The United States is a more religiously diverse and pluralistic place than it was in the founding period, thanks in part to the way the Bill of Rights protects religious freedom. With both history and the future in mind, the founding generation protected religious freedom as our first freedom. Religious liberty is secured by the First Amendment's guarantee that "Congress shall make no law respecting an establishment of religion, or prohibiting the free exercise thereof." Both these protections—*for* the free exercise of religion and *against* its establishment by government—are essential to ensuring religious freedom in a pluralistic society.

But just how much pluralism did the framers envision when they wrote the First Amendment? Were they writing for a multiplicity of religious expressions or primarily for the multiple Protestant Christian sects and denominations that were most prominent during that period?

In *Endowed by Our Creator: The Birth of Religious Freedom in America*, Constitutional law professor Michael Meyerson writes about how at our nation's founding, religious freedom, religious liberty, and pluralism were inextricably linked. He writes, "The fundamental paradox of America's history of religion and government is that while the individual states began as narrowly focused, religiously homogeneous communities, the United States was born a pluralistic nation made up of multiple religious groups. The religious diversity of the country, combined with the powerful direction of the early national leaders, permitted the creation of a distinctly American concept of religious freedom."

History and context help explain our continuing struggle to defend these religious freedom principles against the insidious ideology of Christian nationalism. Religious diversity looked much different in the eighteenth century than it does in the twenty-first. When the first census was taken in 1790, Catholics made up about 1 percent of the population. When Washington wrote to the Touro Synagogue that same year, the Jewish population in the country was estimated to be between 2,000 and 2,500—a minuscule percentage of the approximately 3.9 million Americans counted that year. The Jewish population in the United States didn't grow substantially until the 1880s, when there was a large migration from Eastern Europe, Russia, and what is now the former Soviet Union.

In fact, in addition to the Christian nation myth, we need to address another myth. This one says that the framers were as interested in the rights of Hindus and Muslims and Jews as they were in the freedom of different denominations of Christians. "And that's just not true": this bold statement caught me off guard. It came from Sahar Aziz, a distinguished professor of law at Rutgers University who specializes in the intersection of national security, race, religion, and civil rights, with a focus on the adverse impact of national security laws and policies on racial, religious, and ethnic minorities. We first met when we were law students at the University of Texas School of Law, and we were talking about how the First Amendment protects religious freedom. I have always known her to be a truth-teller, and her interpretation of our founding generation's intention when it comes to pluralism and religious freedom differs somewhat from other perspectives offered here. She offered a counterpoint to many of my long-held assumptions, and for that, I am grateful.

"The First Amendment was not conceived of in a context like today, where you literally have people of different religions living together and having to figure out how we set rules and have a system in place that allows us to coexist and not force each other to follow each other's religions or punish each other for not following each other's religions," Aziz told me. "These are completely different contexts."

Aziz's perspective is important to consider because it complicates a triumphant narrative of religious freedom. Though they talked in grandiose terms about religious freedom, the framers did not have our current reality in mind when they drafted these principles. By confining citizenship to white persons when the overwhelming majority of the existing population was white Protestant, they were effectively limiting the potential religious diversity that they would allow to have access to the promise of religious freedom.

Aziz explained that ensuring religious freedom has always required advocacy by those who were trying to realize the rights promised in the Constitution. "Testing religious liberty norms comes from the early 1900s onward, in large part in the courts and to some extent in politics," she told me. "The reality is that religious liberty isn't expanded to other groups out of the kindness of the hearts of those who are in control," she said.

Protections of faith freedom have been challenged in the courts over the years, and working out the balancing of rights in a pluralistic society is often not easy. In the US Supreme Court's *McCreary County v. American Civil Liberties Union of Kentucky* decision on June 27, 2005, Justice Sandra Day O'Connor, in a concurring opinion, wrote eloquently about the importance of protecting religious liberty and pluralism. At issue in *McCreary* was the constitutionality of the display of the Ten Commandments on public land, specifically in courthouses in Kentucky. The Supreme Court ruled that the display was unconstitutional.

"Reasonable minds can disagree about how to apply the Religion Clauses in a given case," Justice O'Connor wrote. "But the goal of the Clauses is clear: To carry out the Founders' plan of preserving religious liberty to the fullest extent possible in a pluralistic society."

"By enforcing the Clauses, we have kept religion a matter for the individual conscience, not for the prosecutor or bureaucrat," she continued. "At a time when we see around the world the violent consequences of the assumption of religious authority by government, Americans may count themselves fortunate: Our regard for constitutional boundaries has protected us from similar travails, while allowing private religious exercise to flourish. . . . Those who would renegotiate the boundaries between church and state must therefore answer a difficult question: Why would we trade a system that has served us so well for one that has served others so poorly?"

Rabbi David Saperstein, the former US ambassador-at-large for international religious freedom and the first non-Christian to hold the position, is both an expert in the religion clauses of the First Amendment and an experienced observer of religious freedom around the world today. He is one of the most prominent Jewish leaders in the United States and has been one of my closest allies in countering Christian nationalism for years. I talked with him about how the United States has protected religious freedom for religious minorities compared with other countries around the world.

"The Constitution created for the first time in human history a political structure in which there was a promise that one's rights as a citizen would not depend on their religious beliefs, religious identity, or religious peaceful practices— and like all promises, it has not always been realized," Rabbi Saperstein told me. "Nonetheless, the experience for many minority religious groups in America has been far different than anywhere else, particularly since the 1940s, with the growing affirmation of the court of the rights of all kinds of protected classes."

But we must beware of "a new myth on America that somehow the separation of church and state is anti-God and anti-religion, when it's been exactly that wall that's kept government out of religion. The separation has allowed religion in America to grow in diversity and strength that is unmatched anywhere in the democratic world today," he said. "Even with dropping rates of belief in God, going regularly to worship, and holding religious values central to their lives, there are probably more religions in America than any country in the history of the world, and we accept that as something to cherish in America."

As Professor Aziz, Justice O'Connor, and Ambassador Saperstein point out, the constitutional and legal protections for the separation of church and state are only as good as our vigilance in protecting these freedoms. In the face of expanding diversity and the growing opposition to that diversity, we need to recommit to the constitutional promise of religious liberty. The best way to protect everyone's freedom to exercise their religion is to make sure the government stays neutral with regard to religion and its practice. Staying true to the purposes of the First Amendment now, when those principles are being challenged, is as important as ever.

WE THE PEOPLE

Unfortunately, over the past several years, the US Supreme Court has issued a series of decisions that have weakened legal protections for the separation of church and state. One such case is the *Greece v. Galloway* decision from 2014. In that case out of Greece, New York, two residents, one an atheist and one Jewish, challenged the town board's practice of having clergy lead citizens in prayer during its municipal meetings. The residents argued that the practice violated the "no establishment" clause of the US Constitution. In a 5–4 decision written by Justice Anthony Kennedy, the Court disagreed and found the practice to be constitutional. Justice Kennedy reasoned that the practice in the town of Greece was similar in kind to the practice that Congress and state legislative bodies had of opening their sessions with a prayer. He therefore extended those prior precedents to apply in the case of city council and town board meetings.

Over the past decade, the Supreme Court has also eroded long-standing protections against direct funding of religion, upheld the constitutionality of a forty-foot cross on government land, and issued a confusing decision that has thrown into question long-settled law against government-sponsored religious exercise in public schools.

It is important to remember that, for the most part, if the Supreme Court rules something to be permitted under the Constitution, that doesn't mean it is required. And it certainly does not mean that such a ruling actually protects religious freedom.

Take prayer before town meetings. Justice Elena Kagan wrote a passionate dissenting opinion in *Greece v. Galloway* in which, among other arguments, she explained the impact that these predominantly Christian prayers have on members of the community who don't share the religion of those leading the prayers:

> Let's say that a Muslim citizen of Greece goes before the Board to share her views on policy or request some permit. Maybe she wants the Board to put up a traffic light at a dangerous intersection; or maybe she needs a zoning variance to build an addition on her home. But just before she gets to say her piece, a minister deputized by the Town asks

her to pray "in the name of God's only son Jesus Christ." She must think—it is hardly paranoia, but only the truth—that Christian worship has become entwined with local governance. And now she faces a choice—to pray alongside the majority as one of that group or somehow to register her deeply felt difference. She is a strong person, but that is no easy call—especially given that the room is small and her every action (or inaction) will be noticed. She does not wish to be rude to her neighbors, nor does she wish to aggravate the Board members whom she will soon be trying to persuade. And yet she does not want to acknowledge Christ's divinity, any more than many of her neighbors would want to deny that tenet. So assume she declines to participate with the others in the first act of the meeting—or even, as the majority proposes, that she stands up and leaves the room altogether. At the least, she becomes a different kind of citizen, one who will not join in the religious practice that the Town Board has chosen as reflecting its own and the community's most cherished beliefs. And she thus stands at a remove, based solely on religion, from her fellow citizens and her elected representatives.

Justice Kagan's example shows how government-sponsored religious exercise threatens the promise of religious freedom: equal citizenship without regard to religion. But again, just because the Supreme Court has ruled that cities and towns *can* open meetings with prayers does not mean they *have* to do so.

A better approach, and one that many communities do instead, is to pause for a brief moment of silence. This time can then be used by those gathered to do whatever their conscience dictates. It offers space for religious expression if one desires, without the possibility of marginalizing people who choose not to participate in a spoken prayer practice.

Protecting religious freedom cannot be left to the government alone. Instead, each individual must learn about how our system of government was set up to keep government neutral when it comes to religion. We must allow all expressions of religion and irreligion to flourish, and we must stand up when we see full religious freedom challenged. Our goal remains freedom and not mere toleration. To accomplish that ideal, the government cannot take sides.

READ: Then the Pharisees met together to find a way to trap Jesus in his words. They sent their disciples, along with the supporters of Herod, to him. "Teacher," they said, "we know that you are genuine and that you teach God's way as it really is. We know that you are not swayed by people's opinions, because you don't show favoritism. So tell us what you think: Does the Law allow people to pay taxes to Caesar or not?"

Knowing their evil motives, Jesus replied, "Why do you test me, you hypocrites? Show me the coin used to pay the tax." And they brought him a denarion. "Whose image and inscription is this?" he asked. "Caesar's," they replied. Then he said, "Give to Caesar what belongs to Caesar and to God what belongs to God." When they heard this they were astonished, and they departed (Matt. 22:15–22).

REFLECT AND ACT: What are some of your assumptions about the separation of church and state? How have your opinions been shaped by the Christian nation mythology or a mythology of religious diversity at the founding? What benefits do you see of an institutional separation between religion and government to both? What concerns do you see? How do you see government officials and politicians misleading people about the separation of church and state? How can you hold them to account?

FIVE

Step Five

Take On Christian Nationalism Close to Home

What I remember most about the ReAwaken America event are the baptisms.

When a colleague and I attended that event at the Trump National Doral resort in Miami in early May 2023, hundreds of people were baptized. The baptisms took place in an inflatable kiddie pool filled with water and set up on a porch outside the ballroom. People wearing T-shirts emblazoned with the ReAwaken America tour logo, various QAnon designs, and Trump gear stood in a long queue, waiting their turn to climb into the pool and be dunked. Fully immersed, they were plunged under the waters by three men, and a fourth man recorded the event on video.

I stood for a long time and watched as person after person climbed into and out of the kiddie pool, trying to discern what it all meant. What wasn't clear then—and still isn't clear to me now, many months later—is what the people were being baptized *into* and why. Christian theology maintains that baptism is a symbol of rebirth in Christ—a way of identifying with Christ's death and resurrection, a reminder that we belong to God. Whether performed on adults or children—it differs, depending on the tradition—baptism is a central ritual in many different expressions of Christianity, an acknowledgment of God's forgiveness of sins, and a public dedication of one's life to Christ and to the Christian community.

Here at the ReAwaken America event, the dunker—*officiant* doesn't seem like the right word for someone who had almost no interaction with the person he was baptizing before they disappeared beneath the water—said no prayer. He uttered no words of blessing, made no sign of the cross. He gave no words of welcome to the community of faith, no instruction to continue walking the way of Jesus. As person after person emerged, wet and generally delighted, they simply walked to the side to towel off quickly.

It was unlike any baptism service I'd ever witnessed. There seemed to be no relationship between the baptizer and person baptized, nor a sense that the public ceremony was the result of any meaningful decision. That's what baptism means in my spiritual tradition: you have decided to give your life to Jesus, you are dying to your old way of life, and you are joining a community of believers who have made the same commitment. When you emerge from under the waters, you are raised to "walk in the newness of life": that's part of the liturgy and the prayers said for the person being baptized in my tradition.

But at this event, there was no liturgy. They were just going down and coming up. Then they climbed out, and the next person climbed in and did the same thing. It was an assembly line of baptisms, with no defined product.

Whatever it was, it wasn't a ritual or sacrament resembling anything in any Christian tradition. It used the sacred symbolism of the baptism for a political and an ideological cause. I found the whole scene quite disturbing.

This example of a religious ritual being co-opted for a political purpose is a rather extreme one. But it points to a larger, centuries-old problem of Christian theology being compromised and sometimes twisted beyond recognition in the service of power. Christian nationalism is both a long-standing, deeply seated ideology and also an urgent threat to democracy. It requires the active engagement in public policy debates by people who care deeply about the issue, not despite but because of their Christian faith. In the next three steps, we will look at why engagement in the public square is so critical now and discuss some strategies on how to participate effectively.

But we would be wrong to assume that Christian nationalism does not impact us closer to home—in our faith communities, social circles, families, and ourselves. Ending Christian nationalism begins close to home. This step will explore why it is so difficult to address Christian nationalism in our families and communities and churches, and it will suggest some strategies to begin doing so.

PATRIOTISM AND NATIONALISM

Taking again our definition of Christian nationalism—the merging of American and Christian identities—gets us to the question of patriotism. Patriotism itself is not inherently a problem; rather, the ways in which it is misunderstood and used to silence dissent and insist on conformity are problems.

Patriotism is a love of country. People express patriotism in both symbolic and substantive ways. Waving an American flag, voting and helping others to vote, and exercising First Amendment rights are all ways that one can express a healthy sense of patriotism. Patriotism is also not forced. One is not *required* to love one's country.

Nationalism is an extreme form of patriotism that demands supremacy over all other allegiances. Inherent in nationalism are authoritarian tendencies that require conformity. Nationalism demands ultimate and unquestioning allegiance. There is no room for dissent or disagreement.

In her book *This America: The Case for the Nation*, scholar and historian Dr. Jill Lepore gives this helpful explanation on the divergence between patriotism and nationalism: "by the early decades of the twentieth century, with the rise of fascism in Europe, nationalism had come to mean something different from patriotism, something fierce, something violent: less a love for your own country than a hatred of other countries and their people and a hatred of people within your own country who don't belong to an ethnic, racial, or religious majority." The difference between the two is stark, she writes: "Patriotism is animated by love, nationalism by hatred. To confuse the one for the other is to pretend that hate is love and fear is courage."

How can you tell the difference between patriotism and nationalism? One way is to ask yourself: Does my patriotism require me to minimize or sacrifice my theological convictions or my commitment to the way of Christ? If so, it's not patriotism; it's nationalism. While our faith should certainly inform our political activism, the mission of the church should remain distinct from the domestic and foreign policies of the United States. When we align our identities as Americans and Christians to the point that there is no discernible difference between the two, we lose the ability to critique the actions of the state.

It's also important to note that not all nationalism is as obvious and egregious as what I witnessed at ReAwaken America. Much of Christian nationalism is more subtle—and thus, arguably, even more pernicious. "In God We Trust" appears on our currency. "Under God" was added to the Pledge of Allegiance that many children say in school each day. Flags in churches that feel like patriotism to some congregants reek of nationalism to others.

The bleeding of patriotism into nationalism can appear subtle, but it is dangerous. At what point do worshipping

God and honoring nations become indistinguishable? How do we know what level of respect for our country is appropriate? Are all expressions of patriotism in our religious spaces problematic? If yes, then how so? How can we stop our healthy love of country from crossing over to a worship of country and hatred of other countries and peoples or hatred of people within our own country who are not members of a racial, ethnic, or religious majority?

To answer these questions, people who belong to congregations should consider what message a particular symbol or celebration sends about the mission of the church and its service to the community and the world. For instance, if the pageantry of a July 4 Sunday replaces communal worship of God with the worship of one's country, then it's a problem. Such services can confuse our allegiances to the point of idolatry and twist our theology to make it seem as if Jesus died 2,000 years ago to save America, not the entire world.

When I joined a new church in 2023, the congregation graciously gave me a hymnal for my home library. I was surprised to find a section near the back of the book titled "National Songs," which included "The Star-Spangled Banner," "O Canada," "My Country, 'Tis of Thee," and "America the Beautiful." Patriotic songs certainly have their time and place, but to me, in this book of sacred music, they seem jarringly out of place.

We can learn from our past and choose a better way to express our patriotism and our fidelity to Christ. These are two distinct parts of our identity: American. Christian. When we gather with the body of Christ, let's worship God together, and let's save the patriotic songs and fireworks for our community celebrations in the park or at the beach.

FLAGS IN THE SANCTUARY

For many congregations, one of the most conflictual conversations related to this question is whether to have an American flag in the sanctuary. A few years back, Brent Walker, my predecessor as executive director at BJC, put together a primer about flags in church sanctuaries that remains a helpful guide, and not just for Baptists. I've chosen to include it here.

Should American flags be in church sanctuaries?

In times of heightened patriotism or in the weeks surrounding patriotic holidays, the Baptist Joint Committee often receives inquiries about the propriety of flying the American flag in church. Should American flags be displayed in Baptist churches?

The short answer is yes, but only in certain places and at special times.

Of course, this practice does not constitute a constitutional violation.

The First Amendment's Establishment Clause bars government endorsement of a religious message; it does not prohibit a church from endorsing a patriotic symbol.

The objection to the routine display of an American flag in the sanctuary is that it represents an act which, for some, including me, raises serious theological concerns.

At worst, the placement of an American flag at the front of the sanctuary can result in "flag worship"—a form of idolatry.

At best, when the American flag is placed alongside the Christian flag, it signals equivalence between the Kingdom of God and the kingdom of Caesar.

Christians know that this is not the case. We are citizens of two kingdoms. We are to respect our governmental institutions and pray for our governmental leaders, but that must always be secondary to our commitment to God.

Faith in God is superior to love of country; allegiance to God transcends all nationalism.

In any case, displaying the American flag in the sanctuary in America diminishes our ability to reach out to non-Americans. It sends an unfortunate signal to believers and unbelievers alike from around the world that somehow the Kingdom of God and the United States of America are either the same or are on equal footing.

Even if it is not advisable to display the flag routinely in the worship center, there are other opportunities to show and celebrate the flag.

Here are several ideas:

1. It is appropriate to display the flag, even in the sanctuary, on special occasions.

These include the day of worship closest to the Fourth of July when we celebrate our country's independence, a religious freedom day when we express gratitude for the freedom we enjoy as Americans, and yes, even in times of national crisis and mourning. However, even then, the flag should be positioned in a way that does not signify equivalence with the Kingdom of God.

2. It is also fitting to display the American flag along with flags from other countries. The symbolism would signify unity with Christians throughout the world, appropriately displayed on World Communion Sunday, for example.

3. The flag can be displayed routinely in other parts of the church campus not devoted to the worship of God. This could include the fellowship hall, assembly rooms and other places where it can be seen and appreciated but where it does not threaten to displace the cross as the quintessential symbol of Christianity.

A healthy sense of patriotism is good. But we are Christians first and Americans second. When these words are used together, *Christian* is the noun; *American* the adjective. Our symbolism in worship should reflect that theological truth.

In my dozens of presentations to Christian communities about Christian nationalism, I've learned about how contentious conversations about the American flag and other symbols of patriotism can be. In nearly every session I have led, a pastor or lay leader has shared a story of how a disgruntled member has threatened to leave—or even left—a church when the flag is removed from the sanctuary. These anecdotes show the extent to which Christian nationalism is embedded in our worship practices and sacred spaces.

TAKING ON CHRISTIAN NATIONALISM FROM THE PULPIT

An even more difficult task is to take on the ways that Christian nationalism has shaped our theologies. In step two, we explored how our own theologies have been compromised by Christian nationalism, due in large part to the dominant church's complicity with racism and oppression over centuries.

Christian clergy and other leaders, especially those with access to a pulpit, have a particular role to play in taking on Christian nationalism in the church. In recent years, more pastors and priests have begun to preach explicitly against Christian nationalism. Sometimes people choose to preach on Christian nationalism around a patriotic holiday in order to distinguish our roles as Americans and Christians. In June 2023, Faithful America, an online community of Christians, hosted its first sermon drive to encourage preaching against Christian nationalism around Flag Day.

Others may find connections to Christian nationalism embedded within certain scripture passages or around the liturgical calendar. I heard Rev. Victoria Robb Powers, pastor of Royal Lane Baptist Church in Dallas, Texas, preach on Christian nationalism in November 2023 on Christ the King Sunday. In the church calendar, Christ the King Sunday ends the liturgical year and precedes the first Sunday of Advent. On this Sunday, which celebrates the authority of Christ over all the universe, Rev. Powers saw the connections between a nationalist version of the faith and the true faith that day calls us toward:

The point of Christ the King Sunday is to celebrate that Christ is at the right hand of God and reigns as Lord over everything in heaven and on earth. And I'm not against that proclamation, but I'll tell you: Christ the King Sunday often takes that claim and litters it with hierarchical and patriarchal language and then drenches it with images of crowns and thrones and scepters. . . .

In fact, when I think of the phrase "Christ Is King," I can't help but think of the posters paraded at our nation's Capitol during the January 6th insurrection. I hear this phrase, "Christ Is King," as a war cry against declining Christian cultural power. "Christ Is King" feels like a tagline for Christian nationalism, doesn't it? I mean isn't it the rhetoric for why all American life should be fused with the Christian faith—because Christ is King? Christian nationalism, which used to be a fringe viewpoint, now has a foothold in American politics, and I'll tell you: this church holiday is not helping.

Rev. Powers then shared with the congregation the origins of Christ the King Sunday and offered a way to reclaim the theology from those who would co-opt it for political ends:

> The holiday began in the early 1920s as a response to World War I and the rise of totalitarianism. In that climate, it seemed appropriate for the church at the time to reassert to the world the kingship and reign of Christ which always stands in contrast to all earthly claims of lordship over human life.
>
> Christ the King Sunday was meant to remind the people that, unlike tyrants and dictators or slaveowners, Jesus is the just and faithful one who brings order and peace to the world when we follow his command and love one another. It was meant to clarify for Christians who felt themselves pulled in competing directions that Christ rules in our hearts and our wills and our minds and in our bodies.

Ending Christian nationalism will require that more Christian leaders preach prophetically against it. But this task is not just for those who proclaim from a pulpit; it is the task for every member of a Christian community.

The great difficulty is that the very presence of Christian nationalism in the culture can make these candid conversations in church fraught. What can we do to talk about this force that we see clearly but that those we love might not see at all?

TALKING ABOUT CHRISTIAN NATIONALISM IN CHURCH

Rev. Dr. Austin Carty is pastor of Boulevard Baptist Church, a decidedly "purple" congregation in Anderson, South Carolina. "Our church does have a lot of diversity of viewpoints politically, theologically, and socially," Dr. Carty told me soon after I visited his church in 2023. "That can be a burden if a leader is naive or feels that he or she must immediately try to 'fix' that as if it's something that's broken and in need of repair. But if it's approached from a way that honors where folks are and why folks are where they are and tries to create and cultivate space for dialogue and understanding, there can be opportunities for folks to be enriched in their difference of viewpoint rather than being torn apart by it."

That's something of a tall order these days, when everything is so divided. Dr. Carty says that a church community must try to "learn how to constructively live in that tension and remain bonded together. . . . That's the kind of background framework that I think somebody who comes to a purple church does well to come with, rather than coming in with an idea of trying to draw everybody to where she or he might be. I think we see that happening in both conservative and progressive parts of culture generally and in the church particularly."

In 2023, Dr. Carty had been pastor of Boulevard for four years—four of the most contentious political years in recent memory. Creating space for dialogue where congregants feel safe enough to name the reality of their differences has taken time. He says it's still a process that can feel fragile. Dr. Carty suggested that one of the most constructive things a congregation can do about Christian nationalism is also one of the most time-consuming. It involves helping parishioners of all political stripes distinguish between Christian nationalism and political conservatism. "It can't just happen through one sermon or through one conversation with someone or through one lesson within a group," he said. "One is not necessarily a Christian nationalist if one is politically conservative, but I think a lot of folks who are politically conservative hear 'Christian nationalism' and think it is used by people who have different political viewpoints as a label to describe those who vote Republican."

Dr. Carty says that his congregation includes many people who are politically conservative but don't embrace Christian nationalism. "That doesn't mean anybody is incapable of being drawn into an ideology that in some ways has affinities with their own political viewpoint," he said. "The same thing can happen on the left too. Being able to at first take some air out of the ball with those charged words—by saying, 'Look, these are two different things; here is what Christian nationalism is, and here are the hallmarks of political conservatism; the two are not synonymous'—has been helpful."

Preventing Christian nationalism from establishing a foothold in a congregation isn't easy, Dr. Carty says. Staying vigilant about keeping communication open in a congregation is key: "Evidence of Christian nationalism is so pervasive right now and so deeply embedded in the media structures that we all live and move and have our being in right now. Unless one is completely divorced from the internet, which is hardly anyone, and unless one has no appetite for cable news, which is hardly anyone, then some of these ideas can take root."

For Dr. Carty and other pastors, helping congregants become more discerning about the concept of faith freedom for all is a slow but fruitful process. Dr. Carty said his congregants are beginning to see more clearly "how Christian nationalism is antithetical to the gospel. How some of these ideas masquerade and on the surface might look like things that, using the right 'Christian' language, *appear* to be Christian but are certainly not in keeping with the gospel that is proclaimed by Jesus."

INVITING CONVERSATION
WITH THOSE WE LOVE

The most common question I get when talking about Christian nationalism is something like this: How can I talk to my uncle who is convinced that the United States is a Christian nation and therefore should have Christian laws? Our largest sphere of influence is with those we already know well and have built trust with through years of relationship and shared experience. It is often easier to think about railing against the latest example of Christian nationalism from a national leader or an ideologue than to have a candid conversation with a loved one who espouses some of the same ideas.

One of the most important starting places for conversation is a commitment to viewing Christian nationalism as an ideology, not an identity. As we began to see in step 1, using the language of Christian nationalism—versus calling someone a *Christian nationalist*—provides room for dialogue. As we have defined it, Christian nationalism is an ideology and a cultural framework. It exists in the culture, and we all face opportunities to either embrace or reject it. Some days we may do better than others in the struggle to move away from Christian nationalism. There is grace in realizing that each conversation, each day, opens a new possibility for change.

Seeing Christian nationalism as an ideology—which we can all slide toward or away from on any given day—will ultimately be more effective in countering it than seeing it as an immutable part of a person's identity. Labeling someone a "Christian nationalist" does not create that same openness to dialogue because it makes the ideology a part of someone's fixed identity.

Rev. Dr. Pamela Cooper-White is the author of *The Psychology of Christian Nationalism: Why People Are Drawn In and How to Talk Across the Divide*. She has given many presentations on the topic, including an event at King of Glory Lutheran Church in Dallas, Texas, in November 2023, in which I also participated. She said, "When it comes to a firmly entrenched adherent to Christian nationalist beliefs, we have to remember that we are trying to engage not only with an individual but with their favorite news network, an ever-self-reinforcing bubble of opinion fed to them on social media through algorithms sifting their clicks and likes, and the hundreds or even thousands of members of their church—where they just praised Jesus and asked him to save the United States while listening to heart-thumping rock music and indoctrinating sermons. We're trying to talk with QAnon. So, if you take one thing away from tonight: argumentation will not work. Period."

But that does not mean that dialogue is impossible in all cases. Dr. Cooper-White suggests that we ask ourselves three questions: "Am I the right person to be having this conversation?" "Is this the right time?" "Is this the right place?"

The "right person" with whom to have a conversation about Christian nationalism is often someone to whom you are already connected. Dr. Cooper-White notes that often the best opportunity is "where mutual liking and trust are perhaps already established—for example, with a coworker, a neighbor, a skeptical family member, or a friendly acquaintance. The only way 'in' to such a conversation is to show respect and to listen—not to pounce on an error in their thinking or immediately try to 'enlighten' or 'heal' them." She said we should try to "understand with as much empathy as we can muster what it must be like to be this person and to inhabit their life, with its various challenges and stresses."

In other words, talking about Christian nationalism with someone close to you is similar to talking about other difficult topics: the best approach is humility and genuine curiosity. I have never had much success when approaching a tough conversation with the goal of making the other person see things exactly the way that I see them. Trying to understand how the other person came to the views that they have will open up more opportunities for sharing. You can then share with them some of the reflections that you have had as you have deepened your thinking, maybe even as you have worked through the steps of this book. Being transparent about assumptions you have made in the past and subsequent shifts in your thinking may give an opening or permission for the other person to contemplate new possibilities for themselves.

As Dr. Carty noted, it is often not just one conversation that will make a difference but relationships built over time, with mutual sharing and learning, that can lead to growth for everyone involved.

Broaching these topics in your personal relationships—whether it be in your religious community, your friend group, or your family—may be difficult, but it is necessary. Avoiding talking about Christian nationalism is one reason it has flourished to the extent that it has. We won't be able to end Christian nationalism in the public square if we aren't also attending to it close to home. We won't end it if we aren't willing to talk and listen to those at risk of buying into its logic and promises.

Ending Christian nationalism will take a large and diverse community working together for systemic change. In the next step, we will discuss some strategies for effective organizing and how white Christians need to be cautious not to perpetuate white Christian nationalism while we do this important work.

READ: He gave some apostles, some prophets, some evangelists, and some pastors and teachers. His purpose was to equip God's people for the work of serving and building up the body of Christ until we all reach the unity of faith and knowledge of God's Son. God's goal is for us to become mature adults—to be fully grown, measured by the standard of the fullness of Christ. As a result, we aren't supposed to be infants any longer who can be tossed and blown around by every wind that comes from teaching with deceitful scheming and the tricks people play to deliberately mislead others. Instead, by speaking the truth with love, let's grow in every way into Christ, who is the head. The whole body grows from him, as it is joined and held together by all the supporting ligaments. The body makes itself grow in that it builds itself up with love as each one does its part (Eph. 4:11–16).

REFLECT AND ACT: Ask your pastor if they would preach on Christian nationalism. Start a small group discussion about the topic. One resource could be this book or resources at ChristiansAgainstChristianNationalism.org. Practice having a tough conversation with people in your small group and then try it at the right time and place with someone with whom you are close.

SIX

Step Six

Organize for Change

I wrote this book to offer tools that help people—specifically Christians, and more specifically, white Christians—act against Christian nationalism. Defining Christian nationalism and understanding how to recognize it are important steps in the process, as are learning more about the expansiveness and limits of legal protections. As Christians doing this work, we must also ground ourselves in our tradition, denounce violence, and address Christian nationalism in our own faith communities and family and friend circles.

But if we are to truly make progress, we must take collective action. And we can do so through joining community-based groups: multiracial, multiethnic, and multifaith coalitions of people who are committed to working together for change.

Why? While Christian nationalism is a national problem, it affects people most on the local level. Many of the examples of Christian nationalism detailed in media, including in this book, deal with national examples of people and organizations that embrace and perpetuate the ideology. While these examples help us understand what Christian nationalism is, they don't capture how Christian nationalism is harming people in their daily lives.

Some of that harm is physical violence or threats of physical violence, which we discussed in step 3. But harm also comes in the form of policies that perpetuate Christian nationalism. The adage that all politics is local applies here. Because of our system of federalism, the US Constitution curtails Congress's jurisdiction, with much of the governing authority left to the state and local levels. Christian nationalism is showing up in distinct ways in all these different places. There is no one-size-fits-all approach to solving Christian nationalism. Each community must discern the harm Christian nationalism is causing and work together to fashion interventions—both to prevent harm and to build a more equitable society for all.

If we try to end Christian nationalism without a focused, local approach, we will fail. National statements or resolutions are an important first step but alone will do little to effect lasting change. Ending Christian nationalism requires that collaborative work be done from the ground up.

A MODEL FOR ORGANIZING

Organizing as a tool for social change has had success in a number of different contexts. Labor movements, one of the most well-known models of organizing, use a union model, in which individuals band together to achieve aims such as living wages and humane working conditions. The civil rights movement was a powerful model of collective action, bringing together a diverse coalition of individuals in pursuit of racial justice through campaigns for desegregation, voting rights, and other civil liberties.

While there are various models for community organizing, the one I put forward here as a framework to end Christian nationalism is detailed in the book *Faith-Rooted Organizing: Mobilizing the Church in Service to the World* by Rev. Dr. Alexia Salvatierra and Rev. Dr. Peter Heltzel. As experts in community organizing, Dr. Salvatierra and Dr. Heltzel profile several organizers and coalitions in their book to demonstrate both the theory and practice of faith-rooted organizing. As I write this book, Christians Against Christian Nationalism is launching our first local organizing projects, and some of our early experience helps inform this step. My discussion of these community organizing principles is admittedly cursory, and I intend it only to introduce these ideas and encourage further learning.

What do we mean by community organizing? Dr. Salvatierra and Dr. Heltzel define organizing as "the practice of bringing people together to create systemic change in their community." Community organizing is done from the ground up, not top down. It is local in nature because it brings people together to meet the needs of the community. Organizers do not have a predetermined plan because the people involved in the local coalition are the ones to discern their own goals.

Faith-rooted organizing, according to Dr. Salvatierra and Dr. Heltzel, "is based on the belief that many aspects of spirituality, faith traditions, faith practices, and faith communities can contribute in unique and powerful ways to the creation of just communities and societies." Inherent in this definition is an affirmation of not just religion but religious pluralism. Faith-rooted organizing, when done well, will assemble a diverse coalition of people who respect religious difference and the powerful ways that faith can affect social change. One need not be a member of a faith community to organize with or alongside such a coalition of people. In fact, inherent in the model is an assumption that we will be working with people who are not part of faith communities. But faith-rooted organizing affirms the value of being grounded in and specific about the faith tradition that motivates you. This framework is also then a model for the religiously pluralistic society we are hoping to foster.

Also embedded in the concept of community organizing is an affirmation of community: the idea that something transformative happens when a group of individuals works together. The Christian scriptures provide a beautiful analogy for this idea in the church as the "Body of Christ." In

1 Corinthians 12, Paul describes the church as a body with many parts. All the parts of the body have different roles, and all are necessary to fulfill Jesus's commands left to his followers. When we come to sit at the table of community organizing, we are invited to bring our piece and see how that relates to the creation of a whole. We are not expected to and not invited to solve this problem on our own.

Community organizing is distinct from but related to *advocacy*, which Dr. Salvatierra and Dr. Heltzel define as "the process of calling on leaders . . . to make public commitments to use their power in ways that respond accurately and effectively to the needs of those affected by their decisions." The next step will delve more deeply into the process of advocacy. Advocacy takes place on many different levels. Advocacy organizations employ policy experts to engage in education and advocacy to decision-makers. I have both served as a congressional staffer and currently lead a national education and advocacy organization, so I understand the important role of advocacy in forming effective and just policy. In order to represent their constituencies well, legislators and their staff benefit greatly from informed and integrous advocacy. Advocacy organizations also help mobilize individuals to advocate to their elected representatives, bringing them more involved in the democratic process.

But ending Christian nationalism does not require us to choose just one path. All paths are needed, including advocacy and organizing. Ideally, the different approaches will inform each other. But in doing this work, we must be mindful that we do not take a top-down approach within a local organizing project.

We all have a role to play in ending Christian nationalism, and part of our work in joining local organizing projects involves discerning our specific role. If you, like me, are a white Christian interested in ending Christian nationalism, here are some questions to consider about the hard but necessary work of community organizing: How do we situate ourselves in this work? How do we work collaboratively in multiethnic, multiracial, and multifaith coalitions without perpetuating the very same white supremacy we purport to dismantle? And how can we assume responsibility for figuring out how to act for justice instead of simply asking our BIPOC siblings what to do? Are we self-aware about our power by virtue of our whiteness in this society, and how do we check our learned impulses in the way we wield that power while working in coalition? These are tough yet essential questions to ask ourselves as we prepare to organize.

IMPACT AND RESPONSIBILITY

When thinking about individual roles within the larger collective of a community organizing project working to end Christian nationalism, we need to consider questions of impact and responsibility.

We are all impacted by Christian nationalism, but the impacts are not all the same. People of color, people who are not Christian, LGBTQIA+ people, and people who belong to more than one of those identity groups are those most directly endangered by Christian nationalism. Policies and laws aimed to further entrench Christian nationalism cause inordinate harm to people who are excluded from this narrow ideology. Physical violence and threats of physical violence are a constant threat to people who are relegated to the lower rungs of the caste system perpetuated by Christian nationalism. The toll—both psychological and material—this takes on BIPOC, non-Christian, and queer communities is enormous and irreparable.

White, heterosexual, cisgender Christians are also impacted by Christian nationalism. The fundamentalist Christianity that is imported into Christian nationalism draws the circle of belonging so tightly that it excludes many white Christians based on other identities and values they hold. But since Christian nationalism perpetuates both white supremacy and Christian supremacy, white Christians are still at the top of the caste system created in part by Christian nationalism.

More than fifty years ago, James Baldwin wrote about the lie of white supremacy and the destructive force that it exerts. "I will state flatly that the bulk of this country's white population impresses me, and has so impressed me for a very long time, as being beyond any conceivable hope of moral rehabilitation," Baldwin wrote. "They have been white, if I may so put it, too long; they have been married to the lie of white supremacy too long; the effect on their personalities, their lives, their grasp of reality, has been as devastating as the lava which so memorably immobilized the citizens of Pompeii."

What rings so true to me about Baldwin's words is how the lie of white supremacy has impeded the progress and self-actualization not only of BIPOC communities and persons but also of white communities and persons. If I as a white person have been socialized to believe in my own innate superiority, by virtue of my heritage, religion, or skin tone, how can I build authentic, loving, and equal relationships across lines of difference? Where do I learn from others who look different than I do, speak a different language than I do, or worship differently than I do? How can I be fully human while I am attached to the lie that I am inherently better or more important or more loved by God than my neighbors are?

Organizing to end Christian nationalism provides an opportunity for people to explore the impact that Christian nationalism has on them as individuals and as a community. There is only so much one can understand about this topic from reading a book, listening to a lecture, or viewing a film. Being in relationship with people with similar and different life experiences, all committed to ending Christian national-ism, will help us understand better the systemic problem of Christian nationalism and how it is affecting our lives and those of our neighbors.

Then, building from that understanding, communities can begin to discern the specific issues that the group will address. Dr. Salvatierra and Dr. Heltzel call these "*kairos* issues": issues that "the whole community discerns as key to moving a social movement forward, allowing shalom justice to take room in a specific time and place." This is a collective discernment, not an individual decision. Collective discernment often can be derailed by white people who either are unaware of the power dynamics in the room or lack the self-awareness to recognize when they are steering the discernment. Collective discernment requires faith that the whole body, working together, is better than its individual parts. It requires prayer and reflection. It requires equity and humility. It is difficult but worth it.

Once the group examines impact and discerns *kairos* issues, it can then consider the question of responsibility. Just as the impacts of Christian nationalism vary based on our identities, our experiences, and our relative positions to power, so too do the responsibilities that we each hold when it comes to ending Christian nationalism. In the organizing model, the process of power mapping allows the coalition to determine who holds power, defined as "the capacity to act or to influence others to act." The power-mapping process asks questions such as these: Who has the capacity and legal right to make public decisions? Who and what influence their decision-making process?

While white Christians generally have not experienced the greatest negative *impact* of Christian nationalism, I believe white Christians bear the most *responsibility* in working to end it because we have benefited the most from it and done the most to perpetuate it.

But *how* we exercise that responsibility requires special care. In determining the question of responsibility, white Christians in the coalition might be tempted to take leadership roles, to be out front in public advocacy. This only serves the organizing goals if the entire coalition has discerned it. While a white Christian's intentions may be noble, we must pay attention to the impact on our community. When people of color are willing to share with us the full impact of our actions, it is a gift, and we can learn and heal. We have to prove ourselves to be trustworthy, however—and even once that trust is built, our own actions can easily destroy it. Without careful attention, white Christian leaders, in countering Christian nationalism, could tend to perpetuate the very white supremacy and Christian supremacy that we are organizing against.

White Christian coalition members should also be aware of and avoid white saviorism. This phenomenon, also known as the white savior complex, occurs when white people, from a position of power, try to "rescue" or "liberate" people of color. BIPOC communities are far ahead of most white communities in organizing against oppression. Though the term *Christian nationalism* is fairly new, the ideology and its presence in law and policy are very old, predating the Constitution. Organizers have been waging campaigns for voting rights, immigrant rights, economic justice, criminal justice reform, and more for many decades. Organizers might not use the phrase *countering Christian nationalism* to describe their work, but that might be a powerful outcome of the organizing they are doing.

Our neighbors don't need saviors; they need allies. As allies, we who are white Christians need to recognize and follow the leadership of the BIPOC community in our organizing. We should discern how we leverage the power we have in the overall goal of redistributing that power.

LISTEN WELL AND ACT ACCORDINGLY

In April 1963, Rev. Dr. Martin Luther King Jr. led a nonviolent direct action in Birmingham to protest segregation. The authorities, acting on the orders of segregationist Bull Connor, arrested Dr. King and more than fifty other marchers on Good Friday. While sitting in solitary confinement, Dr. King read a statement from eight white clergymen calling on Black citizens to "withdraw support from these demonstrations, and to unite locally in working peacefully for a better Birmingham." They wrote, "We recognize the natural impatience of people who feel their hopes are slow in being realized. But we are convinced that these demonstrations are unwise and untimely." The white pastors were more concerned with respectability, with maintaining their privilege in society, and with not rocking the boat than with justice.

Dr. King's response to the white ministers was his magnificent "Letter from Birmingham Jail." He talks personally and movingly about why he cannot just wait around for justice to come:

> I guess it is easy for those who have never felt the stinging darts of segregation to say "Wait." But when you have seen vicious mobs lynch your mothers and fathers at will and drown your sisters and brothers at whim; when you have seen hate filled policemen curse, kick, brutalize, and even kill your black brothers and sisters with impunity; when you see the vast majority of your twenty million Negro brothers smothering in an air tight cage of poverty in the midst of an affluent society; . . . when you are harried by day and haunted by night by the fact that you are a Negro, living constantly at tip-toe stance, never knowing what to expect next, and plagued with inner fears and outer resentments; when you are forever fighting a degenerating sense of "nobodiness;" then you will understand why we find it difficult to wait. There comes a time when the cup of endurance runs over, and men are no longer willing to be plunged into an abyss of injustice where they experience the bleakness of corroding despair. I hope, Sirs, you can understand our legitimate and unavoidable impatience.

The white clergy to whom Dr. King was writing thought they knew best how to respond to the horrors of segregation. They assumed their own opinions about the most strategic approach were superior to those of Dr. King and other leaders of the civil rights movement. As a white Christian, I caution myself and all of my fellow white Christians to be careful and to make sure we are not centering whiteness in our response to Christian nationalism. The white ministers in Birmingham thought that nonviolent direct action "untimely" and "unwise" because they were attached to the power system as it currently was rather than committed to a tearing down of the system to redistribute power. They lacked the prophetic imagination to understand a world without segregation and therefore were not committed to the fulfillment of justice. Where are we, even unwittingly, clinging to an unjust system that serves us because we are white Christians rather than working to establish a system that is equitable for all?

In our community organizing, we must learn to listen well to those in communities most impacted by Christian nationalism and white supremacy, and we must follow their lead on both what we are working toward and how best we can contribute to a liberative response. Given the inequities and injustices of the current American legal system, the response will mean a cost to those who currently hold power, which includes us as white Christians. This work will mean that we will often feel uncomfortable. The feelings of discomfort mean that we are moving in the right direction. We will make mistakes along the way. That also means that we are taking risks that need to be taken.

In listening and acting in deference, we also need to keep the overall goal of organizing in mind. Recall the definition of community organizing offered at the beginning of this step: "the practice of bringing people together to create systemic change in their community." This practice can be transformative for individuals, for the collective body, and for the entire community. It can be tempting to rush to action, to look for the quick wins so that we can show progress for ourselves or even for potential funders. But to define our success solely or even mostly by the campaigns we run or the actions we take misses the point. The community itself, which we are building together, is the goal. If we do this well, we can reposition ourselves for more systemic change for many years to come. We must remember that organizing is the long game needed for this long-standing problem.

Organizing works on the community level to effect change. In the next step, we'll explore one area of our society where Christian nationalism is flourishing that impacts every community: public schools.

READ: Christ is just like the human body—a body is a unit and has many parts; and all the parts of the body are one body, even though there are many. We were all baptized by one Spirit into one body, whether Jew or Greek, or slave or free, and we all were given one Spirit to drink. Certainly the body isn't one part but many. If the foot says, "I'm not part of the body because I'm not a hand," does that mean it's not part of the body? If the ear says, "I'm not part of the body because I'm not an eye," does that mean it's not part of the body? If the whole body were an eye, what would happen to the hearing? And if the whole body were an ear, what would happen to the sense of smell? But as it is, God has placed each one of the parts in the body just like he wanted. If all were one and the same body part, what would happen to the body? But as it is, there are many parts but one body. So the eye can't say to the hand, "I don't need you," or in turn, the head can't say to the feet, "I don't need you." Instead, the parts of the body that people think are the weakest are the most necessary. The parts of the body that we think are less honorable are the ones we honor the most. The private parts of our body that aren't presentable are the ones that are given the most dignity. The parts of our body that are presentable don't need this. But God has put the body together, giving greater honor to the part with less honor so that there won't be division in the body and so the parts might have mutual concern for each other. If one part suffers, all the parts suffer with it; if one part gets the glory, all the parts celebrate with it. You are the body of Christ and parts of each other (1 Cor. 12:12–27).

REFLECT AND ACT: Review the questions for self-reflection posed throughout this step, then think about and journal your responses. Learn more about faith-rooted organizing and other organizing models. Some recommended readings are listed in the resources section of this book. Find out if there is a local organizing project to end Christian nationalism already active in your community. Remember that a coalition might be engaged in dismantling Christian nationalism through liberative justice work; just because they call their work something other than *ending Christian nationalism* doesn't mean you won't find common cause. Learn more about how you can support and come alongside those efforts.

SEVEN

Step Seven

Protect Religious Freedom in Public Schools

Before he became a politician, James Talarico was a public school teacher. As a sixth-grade language arts teacher on the west side of San Antonio, Texas, he worked with students from diverse backgrounds. Like students across the United States, his middle schoolers came from households with various religious beliefs.

Talarico, a Democrat, is now a Texas state representative, representing a district outside of Austin. He is also a committed Christian and a seminarian. Studying for a master of divinity degree, state Rep. Talarico can often be found rushing back and forth between the Texas Capitol and his classes at Austin Presbyterian Theological Seminary. "Talarico is something of a theological Clark Kent" is how a *Politico* reporter put it in an article about Rep. Talarico's faith and politics; "the back cab of his truck is his phone booth, the place where he changes from jeans into a suit, transforming from a seminary student into a state legislator."

So in the spring of 2023, when the Texas legislature was considering a bill that would make it a legal requirement to prominently display a copy of the Ten Commandments in every public school classroom in the state, Rep. Talarico had thoughts. And he shared them during a debate in the Texas House Public Education Committee.

A clip from that debate, which went viral, shows him questioning the bill's House sponsor, state Rep. Candy Noble:

> I say this to you as a fellow Christian. Representative, I know you're a devout Christian, and so am I. This bill to me is not only unconstitutional. It's not only un-American. I think it is also deeply un-Christian, and I say that because I believe this bill is idolatrous. I believe it is exclusionary, and I believe it is arrogant.
>
> And those three things, in my reading of the gospel, are diametrically opposed to the teachings of Jesus. You probably know Matthew 6:5, when Jesus says, "Don't be like the hypocrites, who love to pray publicly on street corners. When you pray, go into your room and shut the door and pray to your Father who is in secret."
>
> A religion that has to force people to put up a poster to prove its legitimacy is a dead religion, and it's not one that

I want to be a part of. It's not one that I think I am a part of. You know that in scripture, it says, faith without works is—what? Is dead.

My concern is instead of bringing a bill that will feed the hungry, clothe the naked, heal the sick, we're instead mandating that people put up a poster. And we both follow a teacher, a rabbi who said, "Don't let the law get in the way of loving your neighbor. Loving your neighbor is the most important law. It is the summation of all the law and all the prophets."

I would submit to you that our neighbor also includes the Hindu student who sits in a classroom, the Buddhist student who sits in a classroom, and an atheist student who sits in a classroom. And my question to you is: Does this bill truly love those students?

Shortly after his speech before the committee, I spoke with Rep. Talarico about his advocacy. He told me that his years as a public school teacher and his Christian faith meant he couldn't stay silent in the face of a Christian nationalist agenda. The Ten Commandments bill was the latest effort by conservative Republicans in the Texas legislature to broaden the encroachment of religion—more accurately, a particularly narrow iteration of conservative Protestant Christianity—into public education. And Rep. Talarico said he had to speak up.

"When this bill was brought forward to the Public Education Committee, I found it offensive as an educator that we would impose one religious tradition onto all of our students, including students that don't belong to that particular tradition," he said. "And as a Christian myself, I found the bill offensive to my faith and tried to articulate that."

When looking at how Christian nationalism is being perpetuated through legislation and policy, we often need to look no further than our local neighborhood schools. Those who have most enthusiastically embraced the ideology, including the Texas Republicans who were pushing the Ten Commandments bill, have strategically focused on public schools.

One reason for their strategy is that, demographically speaking, if Christian nationalism is not intentionally pushed on our youngest generations, its influence could diminish over time. Research has shown that younger generations are much less likely to embrace Christian nationalism than older generations are.

For several years, groups like the Congressional Prayer Caucus Foundation and WallBuilders have developed model legislation for state legislatures to pass bills that, in their words, "recognize the place of Christian principles in our nation's history and heritage." The measures include bills requiring the display of "In God We Trust" and the Ten Commandments in public school classrooms—as the Texas bill would have done—and the teaching of Bible literacy as an elective in public schools.

These model bills attempt to merge identities of "American" and "Christian" by furthering a false history of the

United States as a country founded by Christians in order to privilege Christians and Christianity in law and policy. The groups are explicit about their strategy to target the most impressionable students with these bills. In the 2020–21 version of its legislative playbook, the Congressional Prayer Caucus Foundation wrote, "It is important for our citizenry, especially young students, to be educated about these topics in order to appreciate and understand the principles on which our country is based."

Their strategy has been largely successful. In August 2023, Louisiana became the seventeenth state to pass legislation requiring or encouraging the display of "In God We Trust" in public schools. The states passing these laws have often done so with bipartisan majorities and without much opposition. Such efforts do not always succeed, but they chart the way forward for Christian nationalism's encroachment into our public education system.

Those pushing for more government-sponsored religious exercise and expression in public schools were emboldened by a significant and confusing US Supreme Court decision. In 2022, the Supreme Court considered the case of Joseph Kennedy, a public high school football coach in Bremerton, Washington, who had a religious practice of praying at the fifty-yard line immediately after school football games, including with students who wished to join him while he was still on the clock. The school district had suspended the coach with pay after he continued this prayer practice over the district's objections and even after the district had tried to accommodate his practice by offering other times and places for him to pray—times that would not involve him praying with students. Coach Kennedy sued, arguing that the school district had violated his right to free exercise of religion by not allowing him to pray at the time and place he had chosen.

In a 6–3 decision, the Supreme Court ruled in Coach Kennedy's favor, siding with his portrayal of the facts: that he was offering a brief, private prayer of thanks while his students were otherwise engaged. In his decision for the six-justice majority, Justice Neil Gorsuch abandoned the Lemon test, named after the decision in the case of *Lemon v. Kurtzman* (1971). The Lemon test is just one of several tests that the Supreme Court has used to define what it means to have "an establishment of religion," which is prohibited by the First Amendment.

I say that the *Kennedy* decision is confusing because, if you take the facts of the case as the Supreme Court portrayed them—that Coach Kennedy's religious practice was a brief prayer of thanks while students were otherwise engaged—it seems like the case was merely restating long-settled law. But this portrayal of the facts—that the prayer was brief and solitary—was disputed by the parties and photographic evidence. Justice Sonia Sotomayor included a photograph of Coach Kennedy praying in the middle of a group of kneeling student athletes in the dissenting opinion. Some lawmakers will take the Supreme Court's blessing of Coach Kennedy's prayer as constitutional as an invitation to expand even more into government-sponsored or teacher-led religious exercise in schools. As I lamented at the time, the Supreme Court focused solely on the religious exercise of Coach Kennedy and not the rights of the kids and families. It focused only on the Free Exercise/Free Speech Clauses while severely limiting the Establishment Clause and its important protections for religious freedom.

What will it take for us to preserve the religious freedom of students in public schools? What would happen if a broad-based coalition of people of faith joined state Rep. James Talarico in saying we don't want religious instruction happening in our public schools? How might we convince others that families and communities of faith, not public schools, are where spiritual formation and religious instruction belong? And how can you contribute to religious freedom in your community by speaking up about the proper and improper roles of religion in public schools?

CONFUSION FROM THE SUPREME COURT

For more than half a century, there has been a broad consensus—in the courts and in society at large—about religious freedom and public education. Republican and Democratic administrations have affirmed that religious exercise by both students and teachers is protected in public schools—although in different ways, given teachers' and students' different roles, responsibilities, and power.

Students may practice their religion as long as they don't disrupt the learning environment or interfere with the rights of their classmates. Teachers and other school personnel may practice their religion in ways and at times that don't interfere with their professional duties and in ways that don't involve the students in that practice.

But after *Kennedy*, there are signs that some litigators, legislators, and advocacy groups have taken the abandonment of the Lemon test as a green light to pursue more aggressive measures pushing for government-sponsored religion in public schools. Those of us who are devoted to the separation of church and state should be alarmed—and, more importantly, prompted to act—by such initiatives.

Put simply, government-led religious exercise violates the rights of students and their families to religious freedom. Parents and guardians should feel confident that they can send their kids to public schools without worrying that teachers and administrators will be enforcing religion in ways that may diverge from what those families have chosen.

Religious education has long been left to families and religious institutions, including houses of worship and religious schools. In addition to interfering with the right to free exercise of religion, government-sponsored religion in public schools runs afoul of the "no establishment of religion" principles in the First Amendment. Public school teachers and administrators are agents of the state, often the most meaningful ones in the lives of students. They are not likely to be trained in religious matters, and—just as the case with other government actors—it is not their role to promulgate any particular religion and its practice.

In the past few years, my home state of Texas has become ground zero for the culture wars, nowhere more so than in its public school systems. Texas passed its version of the "In God We Trust" legislation in 2021. Under the Texas law, schools are required to display the national motto "in a conspicuous place" but only if the posters are donated or paid for with private funds. In late May 2023, Republicans in the Texas State House tried, but ultimately failed, to pass that Ten Commandments bill. And that same year, both the Texas House and Senate passed versions of a bill to allow public school districts to replace licensed counselors with religious chaplains, which we'll look at later in this chapter. The Texas effort was pushed by an organization calling itself the National School Chaplain Association, which was essentially gauging how far the conservative majority of the US Supreme Court might be willing to push the legal boundaries of religion in public schools, particularly after the *Kennedy* decision.

During the same month that Texas legislators failed to pass their law requiring the prominent display of copies of the Ten Commandments in every public school classroom in the state, lawmakers in South Carolina introduced a bill to require the Ten Commandments to be displayed in all public classrooms in that state.

My family and I recently moved from Washington, DC, back to Texas. As I was preparing for our move, I had a conversation with my friend Dr. Mark Chancey, a professor of religious studies at Southern Methodist University in Dallas who is widely recognized as a leading authority on the constitutional, political, and academic issues raised by teaching Bible courses in public schools. He published a study with Texas Freedom Network Education Fund titled "Reading, Writing and Religion II," which found that in 2011 and 2012, most of the sixty public school districts in Texas that offer Bible study courses were not meeting a 2007 state law that mandates such courses be fair as well as academically and legally sound.

I could think of no one better to discuss the influence of Christian nationalism on religion and public education than Dr. Chancey, who is a parent of children in Texas public schools. I was about to become the parent of a student in a Texas public school myself, and I wanted to talk to him.

What do parents who are committed to faith freedom for all students in public schools need to know and do in this time? How can Christians love our neighbors and their children well by protecting their religious freedom? And how can we ensure that our own Christian faith isn't being mangled beyond recognition by becoming a tool imposed by the state?

CHRISTIAN NATIONALISM IN PUBLIC SCHOOLS: A STRATEGY

Dr. Chancey and I are both Christians, and it's precisely that faith that makes these incursions of Christian nationalism into the lives of public school students so troubling to us. With all these efforts and more happening at the state level and in local school boards across the nation, I asked Dr. Chancey about the strategy of Christian nationalist groups in public schools.

"Schools are our society's primary institution for preparing children for citizenship. This is where we try to equip and socialize children to function in our society," Dr. Chancey told me. "Public schools are the tax-funded, publicly supported mechanism for doing this. Not everybody goes to public schools, but most children do. So this is the key to shaping the future by shaping the education people get now."

What is the endgame? I asked him. What do people who are committed to Christian nationalism hope to achieve by being involved in public education?

"I think Christian nationalists want to teach the nation's children that Christianity has a privileged position in our society," Dr. Chancey began. He continued:

> They want to do that by presenting an alternative version of American history, one that is inaccurate. They want to do that by teaching about other subjects in ways that reflect conservative Protestant religious beliefs. So they want to, for instance, teach about the earth and biology and geology in ways that reflect creationism. They want to teach about ethics in ways that reflect their own moral values, particularly sexual ethics and family life. They want to teach about the environment in ways that reflect the idea that

God gave the world to humans for humans to dominate. And they want all of that taught from a perspective that reinforces their own identity and keeps them in a privileged place of power.

And what motivates those who want to impose and essentially codify their religious beliefs in public education? "Many of them sincerely believe that this is what God has called them to do," Dr. Chancey said. "They think they have an accurate understanding of history—that *they're* the ones who understand what really happened in the past and what's really happening in the present. So they see themselves doing all of this in service to God. It's a divine calling. They're also reacting against changes. They're reacting against growing diversity. They're reacting against declining religiosity. And in some respects, this is all a defensive measure."

I also talked with Dr. Chancey about the Texas effort to require the posting of the Ten Commandments. One problem with posting religious texts in public schools is that the government is in the position of picking and choosing among religious texts, even within a given tradition. The Texas legislature was using an edited version of the King James translation of the Bible for its proposed Ten Commandments, but as most Christians know, there are many different translations and paraphrases of the Bible. Different Christian traditions use different versions of the Ten Commandments from two different places in the biblical text.

"This bill does a disservice to both Judaism and Christianity," Rep. Talarico explained. "There are way more than Ten Commandments in the Jewish tradition. There are 613 in the Hebrew Bible, and the irony for us Christians is that we follow a rabbi who tried to simplify those 613 commandments into two: love God and love neighbor."

"To tell students that this [the Ten Commandments] was somehow the foundation of America's legal system, which is inaccurate, absolutely appalled me," Dr. Chancey said. He further explained:

> My wife and I will teach our kids about the Ten Commandments. Our church will teach our kids about the Ten Commandments. I'm okay with public schools teaching the students about how [the Ten Commandments] have been important in history, but I don't want them slapping them up on the wall and telling my children how to behave, especially when they do so with a version that takes out the theological core of the commandments—the whole theological context of them as part of an ongoing covenantal relationship. Who are they to decide that these are the Ten Commandments? Who are they to decide that these are the words when you're teaching about the Ten Commandments? When you're deciding these are the words that we're going to put up on every school wall, then you basically have public schools creating their own state version of the Ten Commandments.

A CRITICAL DISTINCTION

When someone levels a critique of Christian nationalist ventures into public schooling, they are not necessarily suggesting that there be *no* religion in public schools. Public schools are not intended to be religion-free zones. Understanding the role religion has played in history, the arts, and elsewhere in shaping culture and society is important, and baseline religious literacy is crucial to living in a religiously pluralistic society like ours. But in these settings, religion should only be taught objectively, without proselytizing or judgment about whether a given religious belief is right or wrong.

"Most people recognize that teaching about religion is helpful and important, and in a religiously diverse society, it helps us understand each other and all get along and try to figure out our common purposes and how to reach them as a society," Dr. Chancey told me. "So I'm all for public schools teaching *about* religion. But I don't want public schools teaching my kids *how* to be religious or teaching them what the 'right' religion is. That is something for my family and my church to do—it's not the responsibility of a public school."

There is a meaningful difference between teaching religion and teaching *about* religion. This distinction might seem small, but the truth of the matter is anything but. This distinction is worth our energy and our activism.

"Religious literacy is teaching students about different aspects of religion—about different religions, different expressions of religion such as sacred texts or art or music, teaching them about different types of religious practices. All of that is appropriate for a public school setting," Dr. Chancey explained. "Biblical literacy means familiarity, at least in a broad sense, with the Bible's contents and themes and impact. In our society, at least, I think there is a case to be made that biblical literacy is one component of religious literacy. What's been troubling about the Christian national-ist approach to this is that biblical literacy has been presented as the sum total of religious literacy: so that if one knows the Bible, that's all that students need to know. What they're saying is what's *most* important for students to know about religion is to know this one sacred text and the traditions that it represents."

"There's nothing wrong with students learning about the Bible in an academic setting," Dr. Chancey continued. "Even reading portions of the Bible in an academic setting and looking at the literary features of those passages or looking at their significance for Judaism or Christianity is OK. The problem is when schools teach about those passages in ways that reflect particular religious beliefs, and in most cases when this happens, they're reflecting Christian beliefs, and in most cases, Protestant beliefs. That's when we've deviated from teaching *about* the Bible to teaching students *how* to read the Bible from a particu-lar theological perspective—which, again, gets us into the sad situation of the state promoting particular religious views over others."

This example of Christian nationalism in the public school context gets back to the core idea of the separation of the institutions of religion and government. The state and the church have different core competencies, roles, and responsibilities. It is simply not the role of government to teach religion. That is the purview of religion and religious institutions—not the state.

But government can play a role in helping expose students to different religious traditions in a faith-neutral and academic environment. "The goal is for students to come out of their experience in public education with a better understanding of their own religious tradition (if they have one), and respecting students who have a different faith background as well as students who choose not to identify with any particular religion or whose families are not associated with any particular religion. Respect across differences should be one of the goals of the whole religious literacy approach to religion," Dr. Chancey said.

Christian nationalism replaces the goal of respect across differences with other goals, Dr. Chancey told me: "The goal is dominance. The goal is privilege. The goal is putting Christianity at the top and teaching students of other traditions and of no tradition that they have second-class status in society."

CHAPLAINS AND RELEASED TIME

When I talked with Rep. Talarico about Christian nationalism in the Texas legislature, he pointed to another troubling bill. Passed and signed into law in 2023, this bill encourages school districts in Texas to start school chaplain programs and even to replace school counselors with school chaplains.

"As someone who's in seminary right now, I know that chaplains do amazing work in our prisons, in our hospitals, in our armed forces," Rep. Talarico told me. "And I'm not opposed to chaplains in some tightly regulated way being involved in our schools. But I can't in good conscience sit here and say they have the same qualifications or perform the same duties as a school counselor."

Dr. Chancey has similar concerns:

> They [chaplains] don't have the training counselors do. There are no actual qualifications to be a chaplain. They could be from any number of religious traditions that are not my own. It is unfortunate to create a situation where vulnerable school children are going to be sent to proselytizers who are not necessarily equipped even for basic counseling. It's a violation of the trust that parents have when we send our kids to public schools—that suddenly there are going to be authority figures from religious traditions other than my own and that children might go to them for direction that might be directly contrary to what we might give them at home.

Dr. Chancey paused and shook his head. "I'm all for pastoral care. I'm all for religious counselors. But they don't belong in public schools."

Another significant legal fight that Dr. Chancey anticipates is the move toward offering official school credit for religious courses taken during what's commonly known as released time. This is a long-standing practice in US public education in which time is set aside during school hours for students to receive off-campus religious education. "I think that's going to explode, and that movement is going to grow," he said. "You end up with the state giving academic credit, potentially, for a course that teaches students that Muslims are going to hell, or that teaches students that Jews killed Jesus, or that the earth was created literally in six days, 6,000 years ago. And you have the state recognizing that coursework with credit. That is fraught with all sorts of problems."

As of April 2024, at least six states—South Carolina, Alabama, Tennessee, Indiana, Ohio, and Utah—had laws or regulations on the books that allow public schools to award academic credit for released time religious education. Christian programs in those states have been the primary beneficiaries of this option. New York City has had a released time program for Jewish students in place since the 1940s, but students do not receive academic credit for their religious instruction.

The credit is the problematic issue, Dr. Chancey argued. "We're going to be in a position soon where schools are having to award credit for religious instruction that doesn't necessarily promote respect for religious difference," he said. "If they've decided that released time is legal, which they have, and it's fair game for anybody—which, if it's legal, it should be—then the solution is for the state to get out of the business of awarding credit for it. That is a line being crossed."

The issue of religious education in public schools, for many Muslim Americans—particularly those who are newly arrived immigrants from Muslim-majority countries—is even more complicated, said Sahar Aziz, the Rutgers University law professor who is also an elected member of her local school board in New Jersey. "Whether they're pious or practicing, whether they're secularized or secular and nonpracticing, if Muslims do not adopt an expansive view of religious liberty, they will lose because they're a minority," Aziz told me. "They really don't have another choice."

"The reality is that the religious education in public schools will be Christian; it will not be Muslim," Aziz continued. "They will not go and teach kids Islam in school. If you have scripture study in school, it will be Bible study. It will not be Quranic study. But because many of them have immigrated from Muslim-majority countries where religion and state are not separated—separation of church and state is not part of the Islamic tradition—for them, they think that it is a social good, a public good, to have religion taught in schools."

Aziz suggests that Muslim parents associate religion with morality and ethics, and so they assume that teaching religion in school is a public good. Many Muslim Americans, especially first-generation Americans, believe, essentially, that any religious content in public education is better than none. For many Muslims, she said, "the absence of religion means . . . the absence of morality, the absence of ethics."

In 2022, in Dearborn, Michigan—a suburb of Detroit and one of the largest Muslim communities in the nation—conservative Muslims joined forces with conservative Christians to lobby local school boards to ban books from the city's public schools. Aziz referenced some of these unlikely alliances and the impact they could have on religious freedom. "These very religious Muslims are working with very conservative Christian groups that have been openly Islamophobic in the past," Aziz said. "That's where it gets even trickier, with the convergence of interests. I want to say, 'Wait a minute, do you realize these people hate Muslims? They're allying with you just for this, but they'll turn around tomorrow.' If the curriculum were to say, 'Let's teach more about world religion and Islam,' they would be opposed to that. So there's some education that must happen within the Muslim community about religious liberty. There has to be an understanding that if you want religious liberty, where you sit at the table affects what your position is going to be."

THE SCHOOL CALENDAR

Sometimes Christian nationalism in public schools is quite subtle. It looks more like Christian privilege, where Christian holidays are prioritized in school programming and calendaring. "It happens when school music programs are imbalanced in their use of religious songs and lean heavily on

Christian sacred music," Dr. Chancey told me. "The courts have made clear that using sacred music can be appropriate, but it's also the case that sometimes school choral programs are imbalanced in their approach. All of these send the message to other students that they are lesser citizens."

Aziz maintains that Christian nationalism is "absolutely the default of the United States." She told me that it might be better called "Protestant nationalism" in some cases and "Judeo-Christian nationalism" in others. She offers as an example a recent discussion she introduced to her local school board about days off in the school calendar. Currently, students and teachers are off from school for Christian and Jewish holidays such as Christmas, Easter, Rosh Hashanah, and Yom Kippur. There are religious equivalents to those major religious holidays in Islam and Hindu traditions, but those holidays aren't considered in the public school calendar.

Aziz said she "knew better" than to even suggest more days off to coincide with religious celebrations outside of Christianity or Judaism. But as a school board member, she asked the board to discuss whether something could be done to symbolically recognize students' different religious experiences. Perhaps she said, the school district could find a way to schedule teacher training days so that students could have off school to mark the two major Muslim festivals of Eid Al-Fitr and Eid Al-Adha as well as Diwali, one of the largest Hindu celebrations of any given year. Could Muslim and Hindu students experience what their Christian and Jewish peers experience: not having to worry about missing school and having to make up an exam or a class if they celebrate a religious holiday? And does spring break *need* to coincide with Easter and Passover? Or could it be earlier in March, when it might coincide with college and university breaks so families with children in both could vacation together?

"The amount of pushback I got was remarkable," Aziz said. "It wasn't, 'No, they don't deserve it.' It was, 'Well, this is really not reasonable. It's not feasible. There are a lot of limitations. It's very inconvenient. It's going to cause us to have to redo things, and so it's an undue burden.' They weren't making legal claims. It was more, 'Well, you can celebrate it all you want, but we can't change for you,'" she said.

WHAT WE CAN DO

Understanding the threat of Christian nationalism in public schools—to families from all religious traditions and to those who don't claim a religious identity—is the first step to advocacy. The next step is to make your opinion known to your elected representatives, whether in your state legislature or at your local school board.

In the case of both the Ten Commandments bill and implementation of the school chaplain law, I have seen the power of advocacy from a diverse coalition that includes Christian voices. While the Texas Senate quickly passed the Ten Commandments bill in 2023, the legislation stalled in the House, in part due to strong opposition from people of all faiths and none. At the House Public Education Committee at which Rep. Talarico spoke, four times as many people publicly testified against the bill as for it, and ten times as many people noted their opposition to the bill in writing compared with those who noted their support for it.

If you live in or close to your state capital, you can make plans to be present for committee debates of bills and register to testify against problematic pieces of legislation. Even if testifying in person is not feasible for you, you can write to or call your elected representatives to let them know your position on a bill. Christians have an important role to play in opposing these measures. Because these bills are often pushed as "pro-faith" or "pro-Christian," sharing why you *as a Christian* are concerned about the religious freedom implications of the proposals may be particularly powerful to the legislators with whom you are communicating.

The night before the Texas House hearing on the Ten Commandments bill, an advocate in Waco reached out to one of my colleagues at BJC to ask how to oppose the bill. She had already emailed her local representative and posted an article on social media about her strong opposition to the bill. My colleague encouraged her to turn her individual letter into a petition and invite other Texans to sign it. In about twelve hours, she had more than 250 Texans join her on the petition opposing the Ten Commandments bill. She submitted it electronically to the committee, and she also traveled to Austin the day after the hearing to meet with committee members and hand-deliver the letter to them.

Even with all these tactics, some bad policies will become law. But our advocacy efforts do not stop there. There are opportunities to advocate before school boards as well. In the case of the school chaplain law, school boards across Texas had six months to vote on whether to adopt a school chaplain policy. People of faith quickly mobilized to explain to school boards why enacting a school chaplain policy would harm religious freedom in their communities. A group of professional chaplains in the state of Texas wrote an open letter to school boards, explaining why public schools are the wrong context for chaplaincy. Their letter was covered by more than forty news outlets across the state of Texas in September 2023. Individuals also took action by contacting their school board members. They spoke out at school board meetings about why a school chaplain program was a bad idea for their community.

These examples show how people working together, in diverse coalitions, can push back against Christian nationalism in public schools. Those pushing Christian nationalist measures—such as the Congressional Prayer Caucus Foundation and the National School Chaplain Association—purport to speak for all Christians. But they don't speak for all of us. And our experience has shown that their top-down structure can be met by broad opposition from people from a variety of faiths and perspectives.

People of faith can call each other to more complex and nuanced ways of thinking about how religion, politics, and public education interact. We can speak about how we practice our own faith and how we support the flourishing of religion and the reading of religious texts but don't believe that public schools are the proper place for religious instruction. Instead, we leave it to our families, houses of worship, and other religious institutions, including religious schools, to provide religious education. Refraining from teaching religion—as opposed to teaching *about* religion, as Dr. Chancey explained—is the best way to protect everyone's religious freedom in public schools.

Take the Ten Commandments example discussed earlier. You can be for the Ten Commandments—that is, you can believe people should live according to the commandments—and you can be *for* teaching them in church. But you can be *against* posting a government-endorsed version of them in public schools. Public school parent and Catholic chaplain Britt Luby wrote a powerful op-ed explaining why she opposed the measure. She described the proposed poster, including, "'Thou shalt not covet thy neighbor's wife, nor his manservant, nor his maidservant, nor his cattle, nor anything that is thy neighbor's.' Who is this message for, at the end of the day? And why? And who is charged with teaching these kids what all the words even mean? How should his Muslim classmate, Ali, understand this poster? And how should his agnostic teacher?"

Luby concluded her piece by saying, "*Because* of my identity as a Christian and not in spite of it, that is where I want the Ten Commandments to stay: in my church, in my home, in my heart."

Ending Christian nationalism in public schools will take a diverse coalition of people, including Christians, who are willing to speak up to say that it is not the government's job to teach religion or religious texts. But we know that Christian nationalism is impacting many other areas of public policy and law. In the next step, we will look at how to engage in public advocacy in our work to end Christian nationalism.

READ: But you must continue with the things you have learned and found convincing. You know who taught you. Since childhood you have known the holy scriptures that help you to be wise in a way that leads to salvation through faith that is in Christ Jesus. Every scripture is inspired by God and is useful for teaching, for showing mistakes, for correcting, and for training character, so that the person who belongs to God can be equipped to do everything that is good (2 Tim. 3:14–17).

REFLECT AND ACT: Review the resources section of this book to find information on how Christian nationalism is impacting public schools in your state or region. Get involved with local groups to speak at or show up at school board meetings or state legislative sessions. Contact your elected representatives to explain why you are concerned about government-sponsored religion in public schools, and share your conviction that religious education belongs with families and religious institutions. Write a letter to the editor or an op-ed essay for your local newspaper. Think about how this specific example of advocacy can be adapted for other issues that your community organizing groups have discerned to be areas for change.

EIGHT

Step Eight

Take Your Place in the Public Square

On a crisp fall day in October 2023, I walked across Capitol Hill from the BJC offices to the Rayburn House Office Building, where I would testify for the second time in less than a year to a subcommittee of the House Oversight Committee about the dangers of Christian nationalism. In addition to written testimony, I had a five-minute statement to deliver and then would answer any questions posed by members of Congress.

I felt apprehensive about the hearing as it came at a particularly fraught political moment. The Republican Party was locked in a battle with itself to determine the next Speaker of the House. It was just a few weeks after the October 7 attack by Hamas on Israel. Capitol Hill was even more divided than usual, and everyone seemed on edge. I was hesitant about my role amid this challenging environment, yet I felt a patriotic duty to accept the invitation to offer my expertise on the topic at hand: religious persecution around the world.

What I remember most from that day weren't my own words, however, but the words of two lawmakers whose approaches to Christian faith in the public square could hardly be more different. Both are Christians, and both carry their faith into their work as politicians. That's where the similarities end.

First came a passionate speech by Representative Maxwell Frost, a Democrat from Florida, in the same subcommittee to which I was testifying. At twenty-six years old, Rep. Frost was the youngest member of Congress at the time. He said he "was raised Southern Baptist. I love potlucks. I was in Awana. I got the Sparky Award. I was in youth band for about ten years." As a person of faith, he said, he is concerned about the rise of Christian nationalism: "I know that Christianity is not Christian nationalism. I oppose my faith being used to whitewash a racist, violent, and dangerous ideology." He said:

> Christian nationalism is a form of religious extremism making its way into our policies and undermining our democracy. These extremist actors are co-opting the language of Christianity and religious freedom to push an undemocratic agenda that seeks the very opposite of what they claim to do. . . .

The Bible itself, in 2 Corinthians, actually warns us against this. Paul warned against this. He warned us against people who would preach of a Christ that differs from the true Christ that we learn about in the Bible. That's exactly what Christian nationalism is doing.

I condemn religious extremism everywhere, globally and domestically. We have to recognize the threat it poses to our most sacred freedoms and root it out everywhere. And I think it's incumbent, especially upon us as Christians, and me as a Christian, to be at the forefront of the fight to ensure that white nationalism and Christian nationalism don't see the light of day.

Rep. Frost is a preeminent example of a Christian in the public square who effectively condemns Christian nationalism and explains how it distorts Christianity to violent ends. That day, he bravely used his platform to call on other Christians—including other Christian lawmakers—to lead the charge against Christian nationalism.

Just a few hours after Rep. Frost made his remarks, Rep. Mike Johnson, a Southern Baptist, was sworn in as the Speaker of the House. Speaker Johnson carried his Bible to the Speaker's chair, from which he pronounced, "I don't believe there are any coincidences in a matter like this. I believe that Scripture—the Bible—is very clear that God is the one that raises up those in authority. He raised up each of you, all of us. And I believe that God has ordained and allowed each one of us to be brought here for this specific moment and this time. This is my belief."

These two Christian lawmakers—elected members of the same legislative body—represent two very different ways of understanding the interaction of faith and the common good. While the separation of church and state is the bedrock of our constitutional system, it was never meant to remove religion or religious people from the public square. That not only would be impossible, it also would be bad for our pluralistic democracy. Religious freedom in this country means we are free to bring our whole selves, including our religious identities, into public life, whether that be as concerned citizens or officeholders. *How* we do that, however, is an inquiry worthy of our sustained attention.

So what do we make of these two examples of Christian lawmakers and how they used their voices in the public square on that day? What lessons can we learn about how people of faith should engage in the political realm?

WHAT'S YOUR ROLE?

In the United States of America, people of all faith traditions and no faith tradition have not only the right but the responsibility to engage constructively in the public square, including in the political process and discourse. As we discussed in step four, our system of government is founded on the idea that religion and government have distinct and separate roles and responsibilities and that the best arrangement for a pluralistic, free society is the institutional separation of the two.

What responsible and constructive engagement looks like depends on what role we have in society. Do you hold a public office of any kind? If so, you need to be aware that officeholders at all levels of government are elected to serve and represent all people, without regard to religion. While they are free to share their own religious identities and views, as Rep. Maxwell Frost and Speaker Mike Johnson did, elected officials should be cautious about using exclusionary language that suggests the government favors one religion over other religions or even religiosity over irreligiosity. It is not the proper role of government to take positions when it comes to religion, either supporting or denigrating religion and its observance. Nor should public officials make statements that merge the identities of Americans and Christians as one, suggesting that to be a full or true American, one must have a certain religious identity or hold certain religious beliefs.

That is why I found Speaker Johnson's words so concerning. By claiming that "God is the one that raises up those in authority" and that "God has ordained" every member of Congress, he suggested that the US House of Representatives is a religious body and not a secular one. He merged Christian and American identities—and not just for himself but for everyone sitting in that chamber, many of whom were not Christian.

If you're a private citizen, not an elected official in your community or state or country, the questions are a bit different. Citizens hold different roles than officeholders and therefore have different responsibilities. The US Citizenship and Immigration Services tells people considering US citizenship that should they become citizens, their specific responsibilities will be to "Support and defend the Constitution; Stay informed of the issues affecting your community; Participate in the democratic process; Respect and obey federal, state, and local laws; Respect the rights, beliefs, and opinions of others; Participate in your local community; Pay income and other taxes honestly, and on time, to federal, state, and local authorities; Serve on a jury when called upon; Defend the country if the need should arise."

I want to focus on the third responsibility in that list: what it means to "Participate in the democratic process" in a constructive way as a Christian. Working to end Christian nationalism does not mean working to end Christian expression in the public square. It would be wrong to assume that the antidote to this scourge is for Christians to simply shut up about our faith. But authentic, effective work to end Christian nationalism means discerning carefully and thoughtfully *how* we represent our faith and its claims in ways that don't require that our faith receive special or preferential treatment.

HOW IS FAITH-BASED ADVOCACY DIFFERENT FROM CHRISTIAN NATIONALISM?

Many people—and I am one of them—are compelled by their faith to advocate for their neighbors on any number of public policy matters. I believe that faith-based advocacy, from diverse religious perspectives, can improve our political process and policy outcomes. Faith communities—particularly Black Christian churches, ministers, and lay leaders as well as Jewish activists—fueled the civil rights movement of the 1950s and 1960s, which resulted in legislation and litigation that ended legal segregation and expanded voting rights to previously disenfranchised communities. Diverse faith communities have advocated together for immigration reform, including for the rights of refugee and migrant communities.

The question is not whether our faith can compel us to work appropriately in the public square; it can. The question is how to ensure our witness both represents our own faith and respects the faiths of others.

As Christians engaging in the public square, we should always remember to ground our advocacy in the teachings of Jesus and specifically his teaching to remember that we owe different allegiances to God and to Caesar (see Matt. 22:15–22). Our allegiance to God is always higher and deeper than our loyalty to earthly powers, so our public advocacy should not run afoul of our religious values and obligations.

As private individuals who are advocating in the public square, we should also be mindful of how we use religious language in our advocacy. We are speaking for ourselves or our communities, not as an elected representative for a secular government and not as a representative of God. We are free to include religious language and scripture references in our advocacy, as we deem appropriate, while being mindful and inclusive of other perspectives.

The late Barbara Jordan, who served in the Texas Senate and then three terms in the US House of Representatives in the 1970s, was the daughter of a pastor, and she modeled this stance for the rest of us. In a speech for BJC's National Religious Liberty Conference in 1986, she discussed responsible Christian advocacy. She said that "problems arise when questions of religious preference are introduced by individuals who are trying to appropriate God for some private, some personal, or some political end." Jordan went on:

> In my opinion, the church is forbidden from representing itself as speaking directly with a divine voice about a given public policy issue. The church can talk to its parishioners about what it feels is the proper role on a given issue, but when the church goes out to act, the church is in error if it purports to be the voice of God in public policy. That is where you have the draw the line. You are an individual. If your views are inspired because of your belief in God, so be it. But the church cannot . . . pretend that it has some special or unique aura which other politicians and policy makers do not have and cannot have. That is just not the case. I would hope that in the public arena the church is a better public servant for its acquaintanceship and recognition of God.

Jordan was pointing to an aspect of humility that is crucial for constructive engagement of Christians in the public square. Her words also illustrate the important difference between faith-based advocacy and Christian nationalism. With faith-based advocacy, we bring our faith to bear on matters of public concern. Christian nationalism, on the other hand, demands that our religious beliefs be legislated into law and policy. The passing of such "religious laws" has long been found to violate the First Amendment's prohibition against establishment of religion.

Other expectations for civil engagement include telling the truth, avoiding dehumanizing or otherwise violent language, and not suggesting that people from non-Christian faith backgrounds are somehow second-class citizens.

Engaging in faith-based advocacy is a challenging calling. We will be criticized, sometimes by people from our same faith communities, while we build bridges with groups that may seem like unlikely allies.

WHAT IF PEOPLE SAY CHRISTIAN NATIONALISM DOESN'T EXIST?

Unfortunately, some Christian leaders—lay leaders and clergy and politicians—have used their platforms and media megaphones to dismiss the idea that Christian nationalism even exists, never mind that it distorts the teachings of Jesus or threatens religious freedom and democracy. For instance, Rev. Franklin Graham, the evangelical leader and son of the late Rev. Billy Graham, told the *New Yorker* that "Christian nationalism doesn't exist" and called it "just another name to throw at Christians." He also said to the reporter, "The left is very good at calling people names."

In the same *New Yorker* story, Doug Mastriano, a Republican state senator in Pennsylvania who supported bills that would have mandated teaching the Bible in public schools, rejected the term and acted as if he'd never heard it. "Is this a term you fabricated? What does it mean and where have I indicated that I am a Christian Nationalist?" he wrote to the article's author, Eliza Griswold.

It can be difficult to talk with people about something we see as a powerful force but that they claim doesn't even exist. Some politicians continue to proudly claim the label—such as Rep. Marjorie Taylor Greene saying during an interview in 2022, "I'm a Christian and I say it proudly, we should be Christian nationalists." But others, like state Sen. Mastriano, seem convinced that the best way to deflect criticism is to claim their critics are making up stuff.

This often involves taking the stance of the persecuted minority. Soon after we launched Christians Against Christian Nationalism, Tony Perkins and his conservative Family Research Council featured our campaign on his radio show and in a blog post, claiming it was just another effort to push conservative Christians out of the public square. I was glad we were clear about our unifying principles: that people of all faiths and none have the right and responsibility to engage in the public square.

One of the most prominent Christian voices in favor of Christian nationalism is Rev. Dr. Robert Jeffress, pastor of

First Baptist Church in Dallas, Texas. Dr. Jeffress took out space on billboards proclaiming "America is a Christian Nation," and he preached a sermon by the same name as part of the church's annual Freedom Sunday in 2018. In his sermons, he regularly espouses Christian nation mythology.

I disagree with the views of these religious leaders. But I do not claim they don't have a right to voice their views or engage politically. The problem occurs when leaders like Rev. Graham, Perkins, and Dr. Jeffress claim to speak for all Christians. In doing so, they take up more than their share of the public conversation and suggest they represent people they don't. It is important that the public square remains equally open to all members of our society—people of all faiths and no faith.

If you are accused of making up the term *Christian nationalism* or using it as a scare tactic to silence your political opponents, I suggest sharing definitions of the term used in step one of this book. Over the past several years, there have been many excellent books and articles written about Christian nationalism, many of which I have cited in the resources section of this book, which also has helpful tools for defining and understanding the term.

If your conversation partner still won't accept the term, see if you can find common ground on what the term gets at: the merging of American and Christian identities as a betrayal of both constitutional promises and the Christian faith. Can they acknowledge that God loves all God's children equally, without regard to national identity? Do they accept that all

US citizens are equal, without regard to religion? Do they denounce violent rhetoric that couches itself in Christian language and symbols? If you can find agreement on some of these core principles, the semantics matter less than the concepts.

CAN WE FIND COMMON CAUSE WITH NONRELIGIOUS PEOPLE?

One of my closest allies in the effort to end Christian nationalism these past several years has been Congressman Jared Huffman, a Democrat from California, who cofounded and cochairs the Congressional Freethought Caucus and who openly identifies as a secular nonbeliever.

In March 2022, Rep. Huffman delivered what is believed to be the first floor speech in the US House of Representatives about Christian nationalism:

I rise today to bring attention to a dangerous ideology threatening our democracy: white Christian nationalism. Most members of Congress don't even know what it means, but experts from the Freedom From Religion Foundation and the Baptist Joint Committee for Religious Liberty have studied it for years, and their new report shows this movement was at the heart of the January 6 insurrection. White Christian nationalism fuses Christianity with a rigid view of civic life, a view that true Americans are white, native born, and conservative. On January 6, it was the connective tissue that tied disparate groups together and propelled them to action. It's infecting our government from members of Congress and top officials in the previous administration to the wife of a Supreme Court justice, whose messages to the president's chief of staff leading up to the insurrection smacked of white Christian nationalism. Thankfully, good Americans, people of faith and nonbelievers, are standing up to this violent ideology. I call on members of Congress to educate themselves about white Christian nationalism and reaffirm the separation of church and state.

I recently asked Rep. Huffman what he wished Christians would understand about nonreligious people. "First and foremost," Rep. Huffman began, "that the nonreligious are not immoral. I think there is an immediate assumption among a lot of Christians that if someone is nonreligious, they're to be pitied or maybe prayed for, that they're people who need to be brought back in the fold because they've sort of lost their way, or that they must be sad and lacking a moral framework to ground and guide their life and give them hope and purpose and meaning."

Of course, that assumption held by some Christians couldn't be further from the truth. Morality is not limited to any one faith tradition or even to religion broadly. Rep. Huffman also told me how important it is for Christians to speak out against Christian nationalism: "It's easy for an outsider like me to do, but to watch your religion being exploited and weaponized and bastardized, and for so many people to just sort of go along with it—it's got to be challenging and heartbreaking."

It can be difficult to engage in the public square these days, given the vitriol. But that is precisely why we need more diverse voices to enter the conversation. We need more models of what responsible faith-based advocacy looks like; each positive example of Christians speaking out will encourage more religious people to enter the conversation. We can and must work together with people of all faiths and none to pursue our shared goals. Given the propensity of some to claim that attacking Christian nationalism is to attack Christianity itself, it is even more crucial that Christians undertake this kind of advocacy.

WHAT ARE CHURCHES ALLOWED
TO DO AND SAY?

If you are taking action with a group, including your church or other religious organization, the question of how involved you can or should be in the political process might come up. While religious communities are a vital part of our nation's social fabric, their role in American politics remains hotly debated.

Because of my legal background and work at BJC, people often ask me whether or how churches can engage in political activity. The answers are not as complicated as many might expect.

The first thing to understand is that US charities, including houses of worship, receive special tax treatment from the government. This is based on their unique and historical role of serving the public interest in our society. The specific part of the tax code that relates to these groups is called Section 501(c)(3), which is why such nonprofit corporations are often called 501(c)(3) organizations. To qualify for this special tax treatment, organizations must meet certain criteria—including, for the past seventy years, not interfering in campaigns for public office.

In 1954, a three-phrase change was added to the Internal Revenue Tax Code's 501(c)(3) section as it relates to organizations that are exempt from US federal income tax. The change, better known as the "Johnson Amendment" (named after its original legislative sponsor, then-US Senator Lyndon B. Johnson), introduced explicit protections against the exploitation of charities by candidates and parties. The Johnson Amendment prohibits tax-exempt organizations from participating or intervening in "any political campaign on behalf of (or in opposition to) any candidate for public office." It stood for decades as a relatively noncontroversial part of the tax code.

But in the early 2010s, the Alliance Defending Freedom (ADF), which describes itself as "one of the leading Christian law firms committed to protecting religious freedom, free speech, marriage and family, parental rights, and the sanctity of life," sought to repeal the Johnson Amendment, arguing that it violated the First Amendment. The ADF launched something called Pulpit Freedom Sunday, which urged Protestant ministers to violate the 501(c)(3) statute in protest. Their efforts at repeal were unsuccessful.

Then in February 2017, during his first address at the National Prayer Breakfast, President Donald Trump announced that he wanted to "totally destroy" the Johnson Amendment and its protections, which was an attack on the integrity of charitable groups in this country as well as our campaign finance system. Getting rid of that part of the code could have caused great harm for houses of worship—as soon as a church unites itself with a candidate, it hinders its own independent, prophetic voice. Plus, the Johnson Amendment protects our houses of worship from political pressure from candidates for endorsements— getting rid of it could even turn our 501(c)(3) organizations into virtual political action committees, providing an irresistible loophole for some who would funnel political contributions through churches to make them tax-deductible. A diverse array of secular and religious groups and people spoke out against Trump's effort as undermining the independence of nonprofit and religious organizations, sharing that they don't need a change in the law to pursue their mission. Since that first announcement in 2017, there were several attempts to repeal that part of the tax code throughout the Trump administration. Ultimately—and fortunately—Trump's attempt to "destroy" the Johnson Amendment failed.

Churches may threaten their nonprofit tax status if they engage in partisan political activities, such as raising money for a candidate or political party, directing congregants to vote for or against specific candidates, or broadcasting political ads. But houses of worship are free to engage in many other forms of political advocacy. For example, tax-exempt houses of worship can encourage voter participation and even host candidates to address the congregation if they give all candidates equal opportunity. Churches can create nonpartisan voter guides, volunteer their facilities as polling places, and drive people to the polls as long as they do so in ways that do not favor one party or candidate or tell people how to vote. Churches and other houses of worship are free to talk about and mobilize their members around topics or issues without fear of jeopardizing their tax status. And, if that's not enough, a house of worship can dive into the messy world of partisan candidate endorsements if it so chooses—it just has to give up that special tax-exempt status.

Our democracy is made stronger by the participation of houses of worship in our public life. And our houses of worship are freer when candidates and parties don't use them for partisan political purposes.

I encourage churches and other nonprofits to be advocates, not partisans. That line may not always seem clear. But we've got sturdy models of religious groups working as advocates and avoiding partisanship—models to which we can turn for example and sustenance.

WHAT CAN WE LEARN FROM THE PAST?

Religious institutions, including churches, can effect change without acting like arms of a political party. As is so often the case, history can be a powerful teacher if we will listen. During debate in the US House of Representatives on this issue in 2002, the late Congressman John Lewis of Georgia—who worked alongside Rev. Dr. Martin Luther King Jr. during the civil rights movement—spoke from his experience. "The church was the heart and soul of our efforts because ministers had the moral authority and respect to stand against immoral and indefensible laws," Rep. Lewis said. "At no time did we envision or even contemplate the need for our houses of worship to become partisan pulpits."

While he robustly engaged in political discourse in the public square, fueled and informed by his Christian faith, Dr. King knew that entangling the movement too closely with candidates for public office would jeopardize their efforts. He intentionally declined to endorse candidates in his official capacity. In October 1960, Dr. King was arrested in Atlanta during a student-led sit-in and jailed in a maximum-security prison—a dangerous and potentially deadly place for him to be held. John F. Kennedy, then the Democratic nominee for president, called both Georgia governor Ernest Vandiver and Dr. King's wife, Coretta Scott King, to express his concern for the civil rights leader's safety. Within hours, Dr. King was released.

Many wondered whether Dr. King would express his gratitude for Sen. Kennedy's help by giving the young Roman

Catholic senator from Massachusetts his endorsement. But a week before the 1960 general election, Dr. King made it clear in a statement that he would not endorse anyone—both because he served as the "titular head" of the nonpartisan Southern Christian Leadership Conference and because of how partisanship would impede his ministry. "[T]he role that is mine in the emerging social order of the South and America demands that I remain nonpartisan," he wrote. "[D]evoid of partisan political attachments, I am free to be critical of both parties when necessary."

Perhaps Dr. King also knew the divisive impact any official endorsement by him might have on the diverse coalition he was building for the civil rights movement. Dr. King needed to unite many disparate factions in an all-inclusive spirit. And he did just that, mobilizing a generation to action and inspiring future generations of activists to this day.

Dr. King did, however, make statements indicating his private support for Sen. Kennedy, as pastors and other non-profit leaders are allowed to do without jeopardizing the tax-exempt status of their organizations. Sen. Kennedy's religious identity as a Catholic was a pivotal issue for many voters but not for Dr. King. "I never intend to be a religious bigot. I never intend to reject a man running for President of the United States just because he is a Catholic," Dr. King said. "Religious bigotry is as immoral, un-democratic, un-American, and un-Christian as racial bigotry."

Dr. King understood that defending religious liberty was critical to protecting civil rights for everyone and that an independent and inclusive church could be a unifying force for change in the world through social action. Dr. King and those who worked with him in the civil rights movement also understood the cost that their advocacy could exact.

It takes courage to speak out against injustice to those in power and those who feel like they will lose when equality is extended to all. If you are living in a community where Christian nationalism is the dominant expression of Christianity, the cost will likely be higher than if you are "preaching to the choir" in a community where Christian nationalism does not hold the same amount of sway. You may feel the impact even more in your private circles, such as your church community, friend group, or family. Finding a community of people who can support you in your advocacy will help you during the difficult times that will undoubtedly come.

In 1857, Frederick Douglass said, "Power concedes nothing without a demand." Ending Christian nationalism means speaking truth to power to redistribute that power in a more equitable way.

READ: Jesus went to Nazareth, where he had been raised. On the Sabbath he went to the synagogue as he normally did and stood up to read. The synagogue assistant gave him the scroll from the prophet Isaiah. He unrolled the scroll and found the place where it was written:

The Spirit of the Lord is upon me,
because the Lord has anointed me.

He has sent me to preach good news to the poor,

to proclaim release to the prisoners

and recovery of sight to the blind,

to liberate the oppressed,

and to proclaim the year of the Lord's favor.

He rolled up the scroll, gave it back to the synagogue assistant, and sat down. Every eye in the synagogue was fixed on him (Luke 4:16–20).

REFLECT AND ACT: Where are you seeing Christian nationalism negatively impact your community? How can you use your voice to advocate for your neighbors? Some ideas might be writing or calling your elected representatives, writing an op-ed or a letter to the editor of your paper, organizing a voter registration drive or helping people in your community to vote, protesting an unjust policy, or showing up in solidarity to stand with your neighbors.

Conclusion

Envisioning a World without

Christian Nationalism

If you have read this far, you know we will not end Christian nationalism by reading books—even this one! No checklist can promise that if we just do these steps in order, we will achieve our goal. Eradicating this pervasive ideology will take people from diverse backgrounds, perspectives, and experiences working together in coalition to discern what changes are needed in their communities and then taking brave action to see those changes through. Building a pluralistic society in which all people are free will take humility, bravery, honesty, self-reflection, and love. There will be costs along the way: to positions of power we may hold, to relationships we have, and even to some sense of self that we have acquired because of this poisonous ideology in our own lives. We aren't reclaiming, restoring, or rebuilding American democracy or the Christian religion; we are together creating something that has never before existed.

When I speak about Christian nationalism to groups, someone usually asks: What gives you hope? It is a fair inquiry, given how dire the information is that I often present. I don't have a standard answer, but it usually involves the inspiration I have received from the people I have met along the way who are joining us on this difficult path. By reading this book, you are one of those people, and I thank you.

Theologically speaking, when looking for hope, I return to the words of the Lord's Prayer as found in Matthew 6:9–13:

Our Father who is in heaven,
uphold the holiness of your name.
Bring in your kingdom
so that your will is done on earth as it's done in heaven.
Give us the bread we need for today.
Forgive us for the ways we have wronged you,
just as we also forgive those who have wronged us.
And don't lead us into temptation,
but rescue us from the evil one.

Bringing God's kingdom to earth is not about installing Christian leaders in the halls of power or using the instruments of government to enforce religion. That approach—the approach of Christian nationalism—has led us further and further away from God's vision for God's children. When I think about God's kingdom, I think about a world in which we celebrate the *imago Dei* in each other, where we show love for God by loving our neighbors.

At Christians Against Christian Nationalism, we know we cannot only state what we are *against* but we also have to state what we are *for*. At workshops on the topic, we ask participants to dream together about what a world without Christian nationalism looks like. To close this book and to help us continue our journey, I share a haiku written by one of our participants in Dallas at our first organizational gathering:

Ideals not yet seen
Justice, equity, no fear
Finally arrive.

Together, through our collective work to end Christian nationalism, we will discern the society that has yet to exist. Together we are imagining a world of justice, equity, and no fear, and together we are making that world possible through brave acts of love.

Acknowledgments

In many ways, writing this book has been one of the most challenging experiences of my life, and I would not have completed this project without the support and love of many people over not just the months spent in the writing process but through a lifetime of care and nurturing. I am grateful for the opportunity to recognize them publicly here.

At the center for me is God's love that will not let me go. My faith in God—and specifically God's solidarity with all of us through the life, death, and resurrection of Jesus Christ—has been the sustaining force in my life from before I could remember. In a world that is always changing, the steadfast love of God has been my one constant. I have found and continue to find endless depth of feeling and thought through study of scripture, prayer, liturgy, music, silent meditation, and acts of service and justice.

For the nurturing of my faith, I am indebted to the faith communities that I have called home: Riverbend Church;

Highland Park Baptist Church; numerous religious communities at Georgetown University; City Church of Dallas; St. Stephen and the Incarnation Episcopal Church; First Baptist Church of the City of Washington, DC, and particularly the Education for Ministry group there; and Royal Lane Baptist Church. The clergy and lay leaders at these congregations have loved and challenged me to grow in my faith and have become some of my closest friends.

Educational institutions have opened doors of learning and opportunity for me. I am grateful to the outstanding faculty and staff at the public schools in Austin that I attended and graduated from, as well as Georgetown University and the University of Texas School of Law. Thank you to my amazing friends from these places whose enduring friendships are among the greatest gifts of my life. You know who you are!

Christians Against Christian Nationalism exists because of the dedication of the BJC Board of Directors and BJC staff team. I'm grateful for everyone who has worked at BJC over the course of this project, and specifically recognize the team members not acknowledged elsewhere in this section with whom I've worked while writing this book: Julia Bradley, Don Byrd, Erin Guetzloe, Dan Hamil, Jennifer Hawks, Lisa Jacob, Karlee Marshall, Valerie Marks, Jaziah Masters, Georgia McKee, Ana Roché, Xavier Santiago, Danielle Tyler, Brent Walker, and Devin Withrow.

There is a large community of scholars, journalists, advocates, and faith leaders working on the shared cause of ending

Christian nationalism. I give special recognition here to some of the people whom I have worked alongside and give them thanks for not only their partnership but also their friendship: Jay Augustine, Jen Butler, Shane Claiborne, Pamela Cooper-White, Leslie Copeland, Stosh Cotler, Michael Curry, Kristin Du Mez, Elizabeth Eaton, Nathan Empsall, Rahna Epting, Joseph Evans, James Golden, Philip Gorski, Cassandra Gould, Wendell Griffen, Jimmie Hawkins, Obery Hendricks, Troy Jackson, Robert P. Jones, Khyati Joshi, Nancy Kasten, Brian Kaylor, William Lamar IV, Rachel Laser, Bill Leonard, Jeanné Lewis, Carlos Malavé, George Mason, Michael-Ray Mathews, Mary McCord, Marvin McMickle, Napp Nazworth, Mary Novak, Bradley Onishi, Doug Pagitt, Samuel Perry, Skye Perryman, Jonah Pesner, Mitch Randall, Paul Raushenbush, Amy Reumann, Melissa Rogers, Paul Rosenberg, Katherine Stewart, Chris and Mendi Tackett, Adam Taylor, Liz Theoharis, Jemar Tisby, Corey Walker, Jim Wallis, Andrew Whitehead, Barbara Williams-Skinner, Jonathan Wilson-Hartgrove, and Aidsand Wright-Riggins.

In the writing process itself, I want to first thank my editor, Valerie Weaver-Zercher, who first brought me the idea for this book and has been unwavering in her support for this first-time author. Valerie's thoughtful edits to early drafts of the manuscript immeasurably improved this book. I am grateful to the entire team at Broadleaf Books for their expertise, especially Marissa Uhrina, who was the production editor to take that final manuscript and turn it into the book you are now reading.

I am grateful to the experts and practitioners whom I interviewed for the book for being so generous with their time and ideas: Sahar Aziz, Anthea Butler, Austin Carty, Mark Chancey, Nina Fernando, Julie Greenfield, Jared Huffman, Jack Moline, David Saperstein, and Andrew Seidel. Thank you to Cathleen Falsani who conducted these interviews with me and worked with me on a first draft of the manuscript.

At critical points in writing this book, I asked close colleagues to review the draft and offer candid feedback. I will be forever grateful for their time, attention, kindness, and candor. They each brought important insights and challenged me to make the book more precise and impactful. They were able to do this because they are all experts on the dangers of Christian nationalism. I recognize them each in turn here:

- Sabrina Dent encouraged me to bring more of myself into this book. Sabrina is a patient friend and teacher on understanding how we must reimagine religious freedom if we are ever going to protect everyone's freedom. I am grateful for how Sabrina brings joy to the work and always puts relationships first.
- Guthrie Graves-Fitzsimmons has been a partner with me on writing this book at every stage of the process, encouraging me to undertake it, explaining the process from his own experience

as a published author, assisting in communicating with editors and contributors to the book, leading communications strategy, and generally keeping this entire project on track. I appreciate Guthrie's boundless energy and optimism about not just this book but also the work of Christians Against Christian Nationalism as a crucial piece of the movement.

- Cherilyn Guy shared her peerless and tireless editing skills with this project, as she did with the landmark report "Christian Nationalism and the January 6, 2021, Insurrection." I am grateful for her patience, dedication to getting it right, and commitment to religious freedom for everyone.

- Holly Hollman brought her considerable expertise on church-state law not just to this book but to our work together, which now spans more than twenty years. She is my partner for our *Respecting Religion* podcast and has dedicated her professional life to faith freedom for all.

- Janna Louie lovingly pushed me to narrow the audience of the book in order to expand its impact, while enlarging my own understanding of this topic by introducing me to scholars who have written about religion and the law from different perspectives, including the immigrant experience. Janna has been beyond generous in sharing her understanding of God, humanity, systems, leadership, organizing, and justice with me, often over a good meal or during a long run.

One thing I learned in writing this book is the importance of place to the creative process. Thank you to Sarah and Rodney Macias for welcoming me to Sister Grove Farm for a writing retreat to finish the manuscript in February 2024. I will always think of that land as the place where this book came into existence for me. That symbolism is all the more meaningful when I remember our observance of Ash Wednesday together in the farmhouse, as we contemplated our work to do between the dust of life's beginning and end.

Finally, I turn to my close family and thank them personally for their endless love and support. Bob and Lynn, you have welcomed me into your family as your own daughter through marriage. My faith has taken deeper root as I have celebrated Jewish holidays in your home and your synagogue. You have provided a beautiful example to Robert and me of what a loving, committed, and mutually supportive marriage looks like.

To my husband Robert and our son Phelps, I can never express my depth of love and gratitude to you both. Leading a national organization and writing a book about a topic as charged as ending Christian nationalism takes a toll on not just the person doing it but her family. I know that you have both made sacrifices to make this book and this movement possible. I share everything with you.

And to my mom, Anita, you have been my biggest fan, my closest confidante, and my inspiration for all of my years. You listened to my doubts about the book, read the manuscript, offered both substantive and technical feedback, and shared it with your friends. I could never list all the ways that you have given me a flourishing life, but if I had to name just one, you have shown me what it means to love God through love of one another.

Resources

My hope is that after reading this book, you will be inspired to act in your local community.

You can join a growing network of Christians Against Christian Nationalism by adding your name at ChristiansAgainstChristianNationalism.org. You can also find opportunities for further engagement in your local community, including joining or forming a local group and finding congregations and other organizations with which to partner in the work. The website also includes an online library of continuously updated resources including podcast series, webinars, discussion guides, and curriculum, all available for free download.

Partnership is key to ending Christian nationalism. There are several national networks of faith-rooted organizing coalitions to connect with in this work, including the Christian Community Development Association (ccda.org), Direct Action Research Training Center (thedartcenter.org), Faith

in Action (faithinaction.org), Gamaliel (gamaliel.org), and
Industrial Areas Foundation (industrialareasfoundation.org).
Visit these websites to see if a faith-rooted organizing coalition is working in your area. Reach out in your local community to see what independently organized faith-rooted
coalitions may already exist.

I have cited many other authors and scholars throughout
these pages. For further learning, I offer this nonexhaustive
list of books for recommended reading and group discussion.

Khaled A. Beydoun, *American Islamophobia: Understanding the Roots and Rise of Fear* (Oakland: University of California Press, 2018).

Anthea Butler, *White Evangelical Racism: The Politics of Morality in America* (Chapel Hill: University of North Carolina Press, 2021).

Pamela Cooper-White, *The Psychology of Christian Nationalism: Why People Are Drawn in and How to Talk Across the Divide* (Minneapolis: Fortress Press, 2022).

John Corrigan, *The Feeling of Forgetting: Christianity, Race and Violence in America* (Chicago: University of Chicago Press, 2023).

Kristin Kobes Du Mez, *Jesus and John Wayne: How White Evangelicals Corrupted a Faith and Fractured a Nation* (New York: Liveright Publishing, 2020).

Michael O. Emerson and Glenn E. Bracey II, *The Religion of Whiteness: How Racism Distorts Christian Faith* (New York: Oxford University Press, 2024).

Philip S. Gorski and Samuel L. Perry, *The Flag and the Cross: White Christian Nationalism and the Threat to American Democracy* (New York: Oxford University Press, 2022).

Steven K. Green, *Inventing a Christian America: The Myth of the Religious Founding* (New York: Oxford University Press, 2015).

Obery M. Hendricks, *Christians Against Christianity: How Right-Wing Evangelicals Are Destroying Our Nation and Our Faith* (Boston: Beacon Press, 2021).

Robert P. Jones, *The Hidden Roots of White Supremacy and the Path to a Shared American Future* (New York: Simon & Schuster, 2023).

Robert P. Jones, *White Too Long: The Legacy of White Supremacy in American Christianity* (New York: Simon & Schuster, 2020).

Khyati Y. Joshi, *White Christian Privilege: The Illusion of Religious Equality in America* (New York: New York University Press, 2020).

Rachel S. Mikva, *Dangerous Religious Ideas: The Deep Roots of Self-Critical Faith in Judaism, Christianity, and Islam* (Boston: Beacon Press, 2020).

Bradley B. Onishi, *Preparing for War: The Extremist History of White Christian Nationalism and What Comes Next* (Minneapolis: Broadleaf Books, 2023).

Alexia Salvatierra and Peter Heltzel, *Faith-Rooted Organizing: Mobilizing the Church in Service to the World* (Downers Grove: Inter-Varsity Press, 2014).

Andrew L. Seidel, *The Founding Myth: Why Christian Nationalism Is Un-American* (New York: Union Square & Co., 2021).

Katherine Stewart, *The Power Worshippers: Inside the Dangerous Rise of Religious Nationalism* (London: Bloomsbury Publishing, 2020).

Jemar Tisby, *The Color of Compromise: The Truth About the American Church's Complicity in Racism* (Grand Rapids, MI: Zondervan, 2020).

Tisa Wenger, *Religious Freedom: The Contested History of an American Ideal* (Chapel Hill: University of North Carolina Press, 2017).

Andrew L. Whitehead, *American Idolatry: How Christian Nationalism Betrays the Gospel and Threatens the Church* (Grand Rapids, MI: Brazos Press, 2023).

Andrew L. Whitehead and Samuel L. Perry, *Taking America Back for God: Christian Nationalism in the United States* (New York: Oxford University Press, 2020).

Notes

INTRODUCTION

8   ***An angry mob soon descended:*** David M. Herszenhorn and Sheryl Gay Stolberg, "Health Plan Opponents Make Voices Heard," *New York Times*, August 3, 2009, https://www.nytimes.com/2009/08/04/health /policy/04townhalls.html.

10   ***He proposed "a total and complete shutdown…":*** Jenna Johnson, "Trump Calls for Total and Complete Shutdown of Muslims Entering the United States," *Washington Post*, December 7, 2015, https://www.washington post.com/news/post-politics/wp/2015/12/07/donald-trump-calls-for -total-and-complete-shutdown-of-muslims-entering-the-united-states/.

11   ***That was just during my first month:*** To see my public statements on these issues, see "BJC Says Executive Order Is 'Back-Door Bar' on Muslim Refugees, our Country is 'Better than This,'" Baptist Joint Committee for Religious Liberty press release, January 27, 2017, https://bjconline .org/bjc-says-executive-order-is-back-door-bar-on-muslim-refugees -our-country-is-better-than-this/; and Don Byrd, "BJC's Amanda Tyler Warns: Trump Proposal Would 'Fundamentally Change Our Houses of Worship,'" BJC's Blog from the Capital, February 2, 2017, https://bjcon line.org/bjcs-amanda-tyler-trumps-proposal-would-fundamentally -change-our-houses-of-worship-020217/.

17   ***In the book, the resource is the Truffula tree:*** Dr. Seuss, *The Lorax* (New York: Random House, 1971).

11   ***I also think about the numerous bomb:*** "Nationwide Anti-Mosque Activity," December 2023, https://www.aclu.org/issues/national-security /nationwide-anti-mosque-activity.

18   *"In The Lorax, . . .":* Lisa Lebduska, "Rethinking Human Need: Seuss's *The Lorax," Children's Literature Association Quarterly* 19, no. 4 (Winter 1994): 170–176, https://doi:10.1353/chq.0.0932.

STEP ONE: NAME AND UNDERSTAND THE THREAT
OF CHRISTIAN NATIONALISM

23   *Christian crosses and religious iconography:* For a comprehensive report on Christian nationalism and the January 6 insurrection, see *Christian Nationalism and the January 6, 2021, Insurrection,* Washington, DC/ Madison, WI: Baptist Joint Committee for Religious Liberty/Freedom From Religion Foundation, February 9, 2022, https://bjconline.org /jan6report.

24   *And there were more than a few white flags:* Historically, the Appeal flag was carried by Revolutionary War soldiers, sometimes with the saying "An Appeal to God" on it, and was inspired by the philosopher, John Locke, who in 1690 wrote that when an oppressed people "have no appeal on Earth, then they have a liberty to appeal to Heaven." That idea was inspired by a story from the Hebrew Bible, where in the Book of Judges, the Israelite warrior-judge Jephthah says to his enemies, "I have not sinned against you, but you wronged me by fighting against me . . . May the Lord, the Judge, render judgment this day between the children of Israel and the people of Ammon." For more, see Kimberly Winston, "The History behind the Christian Flags Spotted at the Pro-Trump U.S. Capitol 'Coup,'" Religion Unplugged, January 6, 2021, https://religionunplugged.com/news/2021/1/6/some-history-behind -the-christian-flags-at-the-pro-trump-capitol-coup. In 2023, the "Appeal to Heaven" flag made news again as it was prominently displayed outside the personal office of Speaker Mike Johnson.

24   *"Jesus Christ, we invoke your name":* Video footage from the January 6, 2021, siege of the US Capitol via the *New Yorker,* posted January 17, 2021, https://www.newyorker.com/news/video-dept/a-reporters-footage -from-inside-the-capitol-siege.

25   *"Not everything that is faced . . .":* James Baldwin, "As Much Truth As One Can Bear," *New York Times,* January 14, 1962, Section 7, 38, https://www .nytimes.com/1962/01/14/archives/as-much-truth-as-one-can-bear-to -speak-out-about-the-world-as-it-is.html.

28   *European invaders of this continent:* Robert P. Jones, "The Roots of Christian Nationalism Go Back Farther Than You Think," *Time,* August 31, 2023, https://time.com/6309657/us-christian-nationalism -columbus-essay/.

31   *Accommodators and resisters fell:* See Andrew L. Whitehead and Samuel L. Perry, *Taking America Back for God: Christian Nationalism*

in the United States (New York: Oxford University Press, 2020), 7–10.

32 ***This method of measuring Christian nationalism:*** "A Christian Nation? Understanding the Threat of Christian Nationalism to American Democracy and Culture," PRRI, February 8, 2023, https://www.prri.org/research/a-christian-nation-understanding-the-threat-of-christian-nationalism-to-american-democracy-and-culture/. "Christian Nationalism: A New Approach," Neighborly Faith, December 2023, https://www.neighborlyfaith.org/cn-report-2023.

32 ***"Approve of authoritarian tactics . . .":*** "What Is Christian Nationalism?" factsheet, based on information from Whitehead and Perry, *Taking America Back for God*. Fact sheet accessed April 25, 2024, https://static1.squarespace.com/static/5cfea0017239e10001cd9639/t/5f5b8999bc43fd65e8d28712/1599834522206/What+Is+Christian+Nationalism+%281%29.pdf.

33 ***White respondents who said they believed:*** Stella Rouse and Shibley Telhami, "Most Republicans Support Declaring the United States a Christian Nation," *Politico*, September 21, 2022, https://www.politico.com/news/magazine/2022/09/21/most-republicans-support-declaring-the-united-states-a-christian-nation-00057736.

34 ***White Republicans who said white people have been more discriminated:*** Rouse and Telhami, "Most Republicans Support."

34 ***Recent research also shows:*** Penny Edgell and Eric Tranby, "Shared Visions? Diversity and Cultural Membership in American Life," *Social Problems* 57 (2010): 175–204.

34 ***Such boundaries tend to exclude Muslims:*** Stephen M. Merino, "Religious Diversity in a 'Christian Nation': The Effects of Theological Exclusivity and Interreligious Contact on the Acceptance of Religious Diversity," *Journal of the Scientific Study of Religion* 49 (2010): 231–246.

34 ***Less supportive of interracial family relationships:*** Samuel L. Perry and Andrew L. Whitehead, "Christian Nationalism and White Racial Boundaries: Examining Whites' Opposition to Interracial Marriage," *Ethnic and Racial Studies* 38 (2015): 1671–1689; and "Christian Nationalism, Racial Separatism, and Family Formation: Attitudes toward Transracial Adoption as a Test Case," *Race and Social Problems* 7 (2015): 123–134.

34 ***Research suggests that "adherence to Christian nationalism . . .":*** Samuel L. Perry, Andrew L. Whitehead, and Joshua T. Davis, "God's Country in Black and Blue: How Christian Nationalism Shapes Americans' Views about Police (Mis)Treatment of Blacks," *Sociology of Race and Ethnicity* 5 (2019): 130–146, https://journals.sagepub.com/doi/pdf/10.1177/2332649218790983.

35 ***An extensive polling project:*** Fifty-four percent of respondents had heard "nothing at all" about Christian nationalism. Gregory A. Smith,

Michael Rotolo, and Patricia Tevington, "45% of Americans Say U.S. Should Be a 'Christian Nation,'" Pew Research, October 27, 2022, https://www.pewresearch.org/religion/2022/10/27/45-of-americans-say-u-s-should-be-a-christian-nation/.

35 *But the study found:* Researchers asked the respondents who had heard of Christian nationalism a follow-up question about whether they held a favorable or unfavorable opinion of the ideology; 24 percent of all respondents held an unfavorable opinion and 5 percent of all respondents held a favorable opinion. Smith, Rotolo, and Tevington, "45% of Americans."

35 *"Americans' views of Christian nationalism . . .":* Smith, Rotolo, and Tevington, "45% of Americans," Section 3.

36 *Christian nationalism requires a carefully curated:* "Testimony of Amanda Tyler on behalf of the Baptist Joint Committee for Religious Liberty before the House Oversight Committee's Subcommittee on Civil Rights and Civil Liberties Hearing on Confronting White Supremacy (Part 7): The Evolution of Anti-Democratic Extremist Groups and the Ongoing Threat to Democracy," December 13, 2022, https://oversightdemocrats.house.gov/sites/democrats.oversight.house.gov/files/Tyler%20Testimony.pdf.

37 *One-third of respondents believe:* Smith, Rotolo, and Tevington, "45% of Americans."

37 *"Americans' views of what it means . . . ":* Smith, Rotolo, and Tevington, "45% of Americans," Section 3 (emphasis in original).

38 *The results showed a high correlation:* "A Christian Nation?"

38 *To exist, the Christian nation myth must downplay:* See Jennifer Hawks, "Hiding in Plain Sight: Christian Nationalism's Threat to Faith Freedom for All," *Canopy Forum,* July 7, 2022, http://canopyforum.org/2022/07/07/hiding-in-plain-sight-christian-nationalisms-threat-to-faith-freedom-for-all/.

40 *If Article VI were to be included:* Jennifer Hawks, "How the Constitution's Original Religious Freedom Guarantee Almost Didn't Happen," Baptist News Global, September 17, 2021, https://baptistnews.com/article/how-the-constitutions-original-religious-freedom-guarantee-almost-didnt-happen/#_Y5Usn3bM12x.

41 *Dr. Butler is the author of* White Evangelical Racism: Quotations from Dr. Anthea Butler are taken from a personal conversation with Amanda Tyler on July 10, 2023.

43 *The idea that America is "God's favorite":* "Democracy and Faith under Siege: Responding to Christian Nationalism," webinar conversation with Bishop Michael Curry, Bishop Elizabeth Eaton, Dr. Andrew Whitehead, and Amanda Tyler, broadcast live January 27, 2021, https://youtu.be/QmgWHBoGBi8?feature=shared/.

44 *"Native folks didn't get the right to vote . . .":* "The Myth of American 'Chosenness'" panel discussion with Rt. Rev. Carol Gallagher,

Rev. Darrell Hamilton, Dr. Michael Hoberman, and Dr. Catherine Brekus, moderated by Rev. Dr. Jaimie Crumley, broadcast live from Old North Church in Boston, MA, on May 31, 2023, https://www.youtube.com/watch?v=P7VeV8NRWYg&list=PLr-CsyMCeFqHSyJH7m3U6J3-8cSoOlHsE&index=4.

44 *Threatening their parents with fines or imprisonment:* "U.S. Indian Boarding School History," Native American Boarding School Healing Coalition, accessed April 9, 2024, https://boardingschoolhealing.org/education/us-indian-boarding-school-history/.

44 *By 1925, that number had tripled:* "U.S. Indian Boarding School History."

44 *By 1926, nearly 83 percent of school-age Native children:* David W. Adams, *Education for Extinction* (Wichita: University of Kansas Press, 1995), 27.

44 *"Kill the Indian in him, and save the man":* R. H. Pratt, "The Advantage of Mingling Indians with Whites," *The Indian Policy, Proceedings of the National Conference of Charities and Correction at the Nineteenth Annual Session Held in Denver, Colorado, June 23-29, 1892* (Boston: Geo. H. Ellis, 1892), 45, https://carlisleindian.dickinson.edu/teach/kill-indian-him-and-save-man-r-h-pratt-education-native-americans.

45 *Many children never returned home:* "U.S. Indian Boarding School History."

45 *The Canadian government has started:* Ian Austen, "Canada Settles $2 Billion Suit Over 'Cultural Genocide' at Residential Schools," *New York Times*, January 21, 2023, https://www.nytimes.com/2023/01/21/canada-indigenous-settlement.html.

45 *According to the Department of the Interior:* "Federal Indian Boarding School Initiative," US Department of Interior Indian Affairs, accessed February 20, 2024, https://www.bia.gov/service/federal-indian-boarding-school-initiative.

48 *"You rape our women . . .":* Erik Ortiz and F. Brinley Bruton, "Charleston Church Shooting: Suspect Dylann Roof Captured in North Carolina," NBC News, June 18, 2015, https://www.nbcnews.com/storyline/charleston-church-shooting/charleston-church-shooting-suspect-dylann-roof-captured-north-carolina-n377546.

48 *At the time of the massacre:* Robert P. Jones, "Saving Our Churches from Dylann Roof's White Jesus," Baptist News Global, October 4, 2021, https://baptistnews.com/article/saving-our-churches-from-dylann-roofs-white-jesus/.

49 *"There is plenty of evidence . . .":* Excerpted from Dylann Roof's prison journals, 33, accessed April 8, 2024, https://www.uscourts.gov/courts/scd/cases/2-15-472/exhibits/GX500.pdf.

49 *Roof was convicted in December 2016:* Mark Hensch, "State Prosecutors to Seek Death Penalty for Dylann Roof," The Hill, September

3, 2015, https://thehill.com/blogs/blog-briefing-room/252690-state
-prosecutors-to-seek-death-penalty-for-dylann-roof/.

49 *At Roof's sentencing hearing:* Mark Zapotosky, "Charleston
Church Shooter: 'I Would Like to Make It Crystal Clear, I Do Not
Regret What I Did," *Washington Post*, January 4, 2017, https://www
.washingtonpost.com/world/national-security/charleston-church
-shooter-i-would-like-to-make-it-crystal-clear-i-do-not-regret-what
-i-did/2017/01/04/05b0061e-d1da-11e6-a783-cd3fa950f2fd_story.html.

50 *In a 180-page manifesto:* Tyler Huckabee, "What Role Did White Christian Nationalism Play in the Buffalo Massacre?" *Relevant Magazine*, May
17, 2022, https://relevantmagazine.com/current/nation/what-role-did
-white-christian-nationalism-play-in-the-buffalo-massacre/.

50 *Sociologist Dr. Samuel Perry describes:* Huckabee, "What Role Did
White Christian Nationalism Play."

51 *"Christian" and nearly 19:* Philip Gorski and Samuel Perry, *The Flag
and the Cross: White Christian Nationalism and the Threat to American
Democracy* (Oxford: Oxford University Press, 2022), 107.

51 *According to the poll:* Shibley Telhami, director and Stella Rouse, associate director, "American Public Attitudes on Race, Ethnicity, and Religion," University of Maryland Critical Issues Poll, May 6–16, 2022, https://
criticalissues.umd.edu/sites/criticalissues.umd.edu/files/American%20
Attitudes%20on%20Race%2CEthnicity%2CReligion.pdf.

51 *With regard to the age:* Stella Rouse and Shibley Telhami, "Most Republicans Support Declaring the United States a Christian Nation," *Politico*, September 21, 2022, https://www.politico.com/news/magazine/2022/09/21
/most-republicans-support-declaring-the-united-states-a-christian
-nation-00057736.

52 *A Google trend report of searches:* Google Trend Search for "Christian nationalism," January 1, 2012–July 30, 2023, https://trends.google
.com/trends/explore?date=2012-01-01%202023-07-30&geo=US&q
=christian%20nationalism.

52 *The most likely causes for these three spikes:* Jack Jenkins, "Republicans Keep Mostly Mum on Calls to Make GOP 'Party of Christian Nationalism,'" Religion News Service, August 12, 2022, https://
religionnews.com/2022/08/12/amid-calls-to-become-the-party-of
-christian-nationalism-little-republican-pushback/. Original statement
from Rep. Marjorie Taylor Greene came in an interview with Tayler
Hansen of Next News Network, posted on Twitter July 24, 2022: https://
twitter.com/NextNewsNetwork/status/1551204108471861248.

STEP TWO: GROUND YOURSELF IN GOD'S LOVE

57 *Exposing that is what:* Quotations from Julie Greenfield are taken from
a personal conversation with Amanda Tyler on July 28, 2023.

57 *According to the Baptist World Alliance:* Testimony of Amanda Tyler on behalf of the Baptist Joint Committee for Religious Liberty before the U.S. House Oversight Committee's Subcommittee on National Security, the Border, and Foreign Affairs Hearing on "Faith Under Fire: An Examination of Global Religious Persecution," October 25, 2023, https://oversight.house.gov/wp-content/uploads/2023/10/Amanda-Tyler-Faith-Under-Fire.pdf.

57 *The Association of Statisticians of American Religious Bodies:* "US Religion: Baptist Family," the ARDA, accessed April 26, 2024, https://www.thearda.com/us-religion/group-profiles/families?F=96.

59 *The chorus of one of the most popular hymns:* "They'll Know We Are Christians," words and music by Peter Scholtes, © 1966 F.E.L Publications.

59 *"Which Jesus do you serve?":* All quotations from Jonathan Augustine from Season 4, Episode 15 of the Respecting Religion podcast: "White Supremacy and Christian Nationalism: A Conversation with the Rev. Dr. Jay Augustine," released on February 23, 2023, https://bjconline.org/s4-ep-13-white-supremacy-and-christian-nationalism-rev-dr-jay-augustine/.

61 *"To follow in the way of that one . . .":* "Fierce Freedom," featuring Rev. Dr. Jacqui Lewis, broadcast live on June 18, 2021, https://www.youtube.com/watch?v=9KfCVSrFkKY.

62 *In her book* Amazing Grace: A Vocabulary of Faith: Kathleen Norris, *Amazing Grace: A Vocabulary of Faith* (New York: Riverhead Books, 1998), 88.

63 *White Christian nationalism:* Andrew L. Whitehead, *American Idolatry: How Christian Nationalism Betrays the Gospel and Threatens the Church* (Grand Rapids, MI: Brazos Press, 2023), 15–18.

63 *"Since the beginning of the Christian movement . . .":* "Democracy and Faith under Siege: Responding to Christian Nationalism," webinar conversation with Bishop Michael Curry, Bishop Elizabeth Eaton, Dr. Andrew Whitehead, and Amanda Tyler, broadcast live January 27, 2021, https://youtu.be/QmgWHBoGBi8?feature=shared.

64 *"We—speaking as a white Christian—have inherited . . .":* "A National Conversation on White Supremacy and American Christianity," interview with Dr. Robert P. Jones and Adelle Banks, broadcast live on June 26, 2020, https://youtu.be/QmgWHBoGBi8?feature=shared.

65 *White Christians need to reckon:* "A National Conversation on White Supremacy and American Christianity."

66 *PRRI research showed:* According to a PRRI poll published August 21, 2020, "Among religious affiliations, white evangelical Protestants (72%) are most likely to say police killings of Black men are isolated incidents. Their views are unchanged since 2018 (71%) and 2015 (72%). The attitudes of white mainline Protestants (53%) and white Catholics

(56%) are not statistically different from their views in 2018 (59% and 63%, respectively), but their views have significantly shifted since 2015 (73% and 71%, respectively), when these groups were aligned with white evangelical Protestants on this issue. Compared to white Christian groups, white religiously unaffiliated Americans (30%) are less likely to view these police killings as isolated incidents, down from 38% in 2018 and a high of 44% in 2015. Among all religiously unaffiliated Americans, 26% view police killings of Black men as isolated incidents. About three in ten (31%) nonwhite Protestants say the same." When it comes to the Confederate flag: "Unsurprisingly, some of the deepest divides over the Confederate flag are along racial and ethnic lines. A majority (57%) of white Americans, compared to 37% of Hispanic Americans and only 16% of Black Americans, say the Confederate flag is a symbol of Southern pride rather than racism. . . . About three in four (76%) white evangelical Protestants and six in ten white Catholics (61%) and white mainline Protestants (60%) say the Confederate flag is a symbol of Southern pride rather than a symbol of racism. Only around one-third of nonwhite Protestants (33%) and religiously unaffiliated Americans (31%) share that view. Among white unaffiliated Americans, 37% say the Confederate flag is a symbol of Southern pride." See "Summer of Unrest over Racial Injustice Moves the Country, but not Republicans or White Evangelicals," PRRI, August 21, 2020, https://www.prri.org/research/racial-justice-2020-george-floyd/.

67   *They chose to be oppressors rather than liberators:* BJC Podcast, The Dangers of Christian Nationalism, Episode 7: "Christian Nationalism, Race and White Supremacy," September 11, 2019, https://bjconline.org/christian-nationalism-race-white-supremacy/.

69   *But that's a no-win strategy because:* BJC Podcast, *The Dangers of Christian Nationalism*, Episode 4: "Theological View of Christian Nationalism with Walter Brueggemann," August 21, 2019, https://bjconline.org/theological-view-christian-nationalism-brueggemann/.

69   *So it becomes a question in the United States:* BJC Podcast, *The Dangers of Christian Nationalism*, episode 4.

71   *I think we have to be performing the truth:* BJC Podcast, *The Dangers of Christian Nationalism*, episode 4.

71   *They include: (1) re-centering Christianity:* "Democracy and Faith under Siege: Responding to Christian Nationalism."

72   *"We must stand publicly . . .":* "Democracy and Faith under Siege."

STEP THREE: DENOUNCE VIOLENCE

76   *I experienced a range of emotions:* I reflected on this in "Reflections on Charlottesville," August 15, 2017, https://bjconline.org/reflections-on-charlottesville/.

76   *I was moved by a firsthand account:* Alan Zimmerman, "In Char-lottesville, the Local Jewish Community Presses On," Reform Juda-ism, August 14, 2017, https://reformjudaism.org/blog/charlottesville -local-jewish-community-presses.

76   *What felt most alarming:* Angie Drobnic Holan, "In Context: Donald Trump's 'Very Fine People on Both Sides' Remarks (Transcript)," Politi-fact, April 26, 2019, https://www.politifact.com/article/2019/apr/26 /context-trumps-very-fine-people-both-sides-remarks/.

77   *The oldest victim:* Peter Smith, "Pittsburgh Synagogue Gunman Is Found Guilty in the Deadliest Attack on Jewish People in US His-tory," Associated Press, June 16, 2023, https://apnews.com/article /pittsburgh-synagogue-shooting-ba843b83bf674d2603a07add57 4f13ea.

77   *In the days leading:* Masha Gessen, "Why the Tree of Life Shooter Was Fixated on the Hebrew Immigrant Aid Society," *New Yorker*, October 27, 2018, https://www.newyorker.com/news/our-columnists/why-the -tree-of-life-shooter-was-fixated-on-the-hebrew-immigrant-aid-society.

78   *Bowers's profile description on Gab:* Kevin Roose, "On Gab, an Extremist-Friendly Site, Pittsburgh Shooting Suspect Aired His Hatred in Full," *New York Times*, October 28, 2018, https://www.nytimes.com/2018/10/28/us /gab-robert-bowers-pittsburgh-synagogue-shootings.html.

78   *"And I am thankful for the law enforcement . . .":* Smith, "Pittsburgh Synagogue."

78   *In the week leading:* William K. Rashbaum, "Hillary Clinton, Barack Obama and CNN Offices Are Sent Pipe Bombs," *New York Times*, October 24, 2018, https://www.nytimes.com/2018/10/24/nyregion /clinton-obama-explosive-device.html; and Benjamin Weiser and Ali Watkins, "Cesar Sayoc, Who Mailed Pipe Bombs to Trump Critics, Is Sentenced to 20 Years," *New York Times*, August 5, 2019, https:// www.nytimes.com/2019/08/05/nyregion/cesar-sayoc-sentencing-pipe -bombing.html.

79   *Five months after the Tree of Life massacre:* Nick Perry, "Man Who Killed 51 in New Zealand Mosque Attacks Files Appeal," Associated Press, November 7, 2022, https://apnews.com/article/religion-shootings-new -zealand-race-and-ethnicity-racial-injustice-f815faab23eab0d363cb 8bef9f85d0dd.

79   *A month later, a nineteen-year-old white man:* Ellen Wexler, "What's Changed since the Poway Synagogue Shooting?" *Moment*, April 27, 2022, https://momentmag.com/poway-chabad-synagogue-shooting/.

79   *Before his attack on the morning:* Ray Sanchez and Stella Chan, "Califor-nia Synagogue Shooter Sentenced to Life in Prison without the Possibility of Parole," CNN, September 30, 2021, https://www.cnn.com/2021/09/30 /us/poway-synagogue-shooter-sentencing/index.html; and "John Ear-nest Pleads Guilty to 113-Count Federal Hate Crime Indictment in

Connection with Poway Synagogue Shooting and Mosque Arson," U.S. Attorney's Office, Southern District of California, September 17, 2021, https://www.justice.gov/usao-sdca/pr/john-earnest-pleads-guilty -113-count-federal-hate-crime-indictment-connection-poway.

79   *We see some of these perpetrators:* Glenn C. Altschuler and Stuart M. Blumin, "The 'Great Replacement' Theory Rises Again, Ending in Tragedy," *Washington Post*, June 2, 2202, https://www.washingtonpost .com/outlook/2022/06/02/great-replacement-theory-rises-again-ending -tragedy/.

81   *A common refrain heard:* Andrew Whitehead, Landon Schna- bel, and Samuel Perry, "Gun Control in the Crosshairs: Christian Nationalism and Opposition to Stricter Gun Laws," *Socius: Socio- logical Research for a Dynamic World* (July 23, 2018), https://doi .org/10.1177/2378023118790189.

82   *Political scientists have drawn connections:* Danielle Hanley and John McMahon, "Securing White Democracy: Guns and the Politics of Whiteness," *Contemporary Political Theory*, May 13, 2023, https:// commons.clarku.edu/faculty_political_science/1/.

82   *We were built on the Judeo-Christian foundation:* Samuel L. Perry, "School Shootings Confirm That Guns Are the Religion of the Right," *Time*, May 25, 2022, https://time.com/6181342/school-shootings -christian-right-guns/. Original statement from Brian Babin came during an interview on Newsmax's "Wake Up America," pro- gram on May 25, 2022, https://www.newsmax.com/newsmax-tv /brian-babin-texas-uvalde-school-shootings/2022/05/25/id/1071441/.

83   *It was the first time that support for political violence:* "Threats to Ameri- can Democracy Ahead of an Unprecedented Presidential Election," PRRI, October 25, 2023, https://www.prri.org/research/threats-to-american -democracy-ahead-of-an-unprecedented-presidential-election/.

83   *In 2022, the organization I lead:* Christian Nationalism and the Janu- ary 6, 2021, Insurrection.

83   *They organized events in Washington, DC:* Christian Nationalism and the January 6, 2021, Insurrection, 14–20.

83   *Andrew Seidel, a coeditor of and contributor to the report, describes:* Christian Nationalism and the January 6, 2021, Insurrection, 16.

84   *The Rev. Kevin Jessip made the Christian nationalism:* Christian Nationalism and the January 6, 2021, Insurrection, 17.

85   *And I can tell you this:* Ana Ceballos, "What Message Is DeSantis Send- ing with Religious 'Full Armor of God' Rhetoric?" *Tampa Bay Times*, September 12, 2022, https://www.tampabay.com/news/florida-politics /2022/09/12/what-message-is-desantis-sending-with-religious-full -armor-of-god-rhetoric.

86   *One nation under God and one religion under God:* Martin Pengelly, "Trump Ally Michael Flynn Condemned over Call for 'One Religion' in US," *Guardian*, November 15, 2021, https://www.theguardian.com/us-news /2021/nov/15/trump-ally-michael-flynn-condemned-call-one-religion.

87   *We need more Elijahs:* Livestream available on https://rumble .com/v2n8wuy-special-live-from-trump-doral.html, archived from May 11, 2023. Audio clip also available within Respecting Religion podcast, Season 4, Episode 22, "Inside the ReAwaken America Tour," released May 18, 2023, https://bjconline.org/s4-ep-22-inside -the-reawaken-america-tour/.

88   *It's clear they genuinely believe:* For more on the charismatic vectors of Christian Trumpism, see Matthew D. Taylor, *The Violent Take It by Force: The Christian Movement That Is Threatening Our Democracy* (Minneapolis: Broadleaf Books, 2024).

89   *One glaring example of Christian complicity:* "The population of Germany in 1933 was around 60 million. Almost all Germans were Christian, belonging either to the Roman Catholic (ca. 20 million members) or the Protestant (ca. 40 million members) churches. The Jewish community in Germany in 1933 was less than 1% of the total population of the country." From the United States Holocaust Museum, "The German Churches and the Nazi State," https://encyclopedia.ushmm.org/content/en/article/the -german-churches-and-the-nazi-state, Accessed May 15, 2024.

90   *Anything is acceptable because we know:* Jeff Brumley, "What Happens When Church and State Merge? Look to Nazi Germany for Answers," Baptist News Global, January 30, 2023, https://baptistnews .com/article/what-happens-when-church-and-state-merge-look-to -nazi-germany-for-answers/.

91   *Research has shown that:* Whitehead and Perry, *Taking America Back for God.*

91   *"Refugees from the Middle East . . .":* Whitehead and Perry, *Taking America Back for God,* 71.

91   *It was precisely this sentiment:* Whitehead and Perry, *Taking America Back for God,* 72.

91   *"It's a form of racism . . .":* Todd Green, "Confronting Christian Islamophobia," Berkely Forum, Georgetown University, May 24, 2021, https:// berkleycenter.georgetown.edu/responses/confronting-christian -islamophobia.

92   *In the 2016 presidential election:* Jessica Martinez and Gregory A. Smith, "How the Faithful Voted: A Preliminary 2016 Analysis," Pew Research, November 9, 2016, https://www.pewresearch.org/short -reads/2016/11/09/how-the-faithful-voted-a-preliminary-2016-analysis/;

and Theodore Schleifer, "Donald Trump: 'I think Islam hates us,'" CNN, March 10, 2016, https://www.cnn.com/2016/03/09/politics /donald-trump-islam-hates-us/index.html.

92 **Evangelical support for Trump:** Gregory A. Smith, "Most White Evangelicals Approve of Trump Travel Prohibition and Express Concerns about Extremism," Pew Research, February 27, 2017, https://www .pewresearch.org/short-reads/2017/02/27/most-white-evangelicals -approve-of-trump-travel-prohibition-and-express-concerns-about -extremism/.

92 **White evangelicals continue to harbor:** "American Muslim Poll 2019: Predicting and Preventing Islamophobia," Institute for Social Policy and Understanding, May 1, 2019, https://www.ispu.org/american -muslim-poll-2019-predicting-and-preventing-islamophobia/.

92 **"What we have been witnessing . . .":** Green, "Confronting Christian Islamophobia."

93 **The statement read, in part:** Shoulder to Shoulder Press Release, September 7, 2010, https://static1.squarespace.com/static/5b52431a55b02cf1 0a3f2cdd/t/5f1ee7de3b65cb156b7c3f49/1595860972560/Originating +Press+Release+September+7%2C+2010.pdf.

94 **"This is not just a Muslim issue":** Quotations from Nina Fernando are taken from a personal conversation with Amanda Tyler on July 21, 2023.

94 **She recalled the murder of Balbir Singh Sodhi:** Harmeet Kaur, "A Sikh Man's Murder at a Gas Station Revealed Another Tragedy of 9/11," CNN, September 11, 2021, https://www.cnn.com/interactive/2021/09/us /balbir-singh-sodhi-9-11-cec/.

94 **The gunman, Frank Silva Roque, reportedly:** Valerie Kaur, "His Brother Was Murdered for Wearing a Turban after 9/11. 15 Years Later, He Spoke to the Killer," *The World*, September 23, 2016, https://theworld.org /stories/2016/09/23/his-brother-was-murdered-four-days-after-911-last -week-he-forgave-killer.

94 **He then drove his truck:** Kaur, "His Brother Was Murdered for Wearing a Turban after 9/11"; and *State of Arizona v. Frank Silva Roque*, accessed April 25, 2024, https://law.justia.com/cases/arizona/supreme -court/2006/cr030355ap-1.html.

STEP FOUR: COMMIT TO THE SEPARATION OF CHURCH AND STATE

99 **Addressing Sunday-morning worshippers:** Conrad Swanson, "Lauren Boebert Told Congregation She's 'Tired of This Separation of Church and State Junk,'" *Denver Post*, June 27, 2022, https://www.denverpost .com/2022/06/27/lauren-boebert-church-state-colorado/.

100 **Two weeks earlier, at a Christian center:** Jack Jenkins, "For Boebert and Greene, Faith—And Christian Nationalism—Sells," Religion News Service, August 1, 2023, https://religionnews.com/2023/08/01/for-boebert-and-greene-faith-and-christian-nationalism-sells/.

100 **Shortly after being elected Speaker of the House:** CNBC's Squawk Box interview with Speaker Mike Johnson, November 14, 2023, available on the YouTube channel of Speaker Johnson, https://www.youtube.com/watch?v=ccfGztlcdek.

101 **As my predecessor at BJC, Brent Walker:** Brent Walker, "Top 5 Myths of the Separation of Church and State," *Report from the Capital* 65, no. 10 (November/December 2010): 8–9, https://bjconline.org/top-5-myths-of-the-separation-of-church-and-state/.

102 **"The Senators and Representatives...":** "The Constitution of the United States: A Transcription," Article VI, accessed April 24, 2024, https://www.archives.gov/founding-docs/constitution-transcript.

103 **Jefferson famously responded:** The fact that Jefferson used this phrase in correspondence to Baptists is often overlooked, but it is important (and not just to Baptists like me). The Baptist commitment to separation of church and state was by then well-known. Perhaps Jefferson was recalling words written 150 years earlier, when Roger Williams, the founder of the First Baptist Church in America, opined, "When they [the Church] have opened a gap in the hedge or wall of separation between the garden of the church and the wilderness of the world, God hath ever broke down the wall itself, removed the candlestick ... and made His Garden a wilderness." Quote from Thomas Jefferson from *Jefferson's Letter to the Danbury Baptists, Jan. 1, 1802.* Letter From Library of Congress, https://www.loc.gov/loc/lcib/9806/danpre.html, accessed April 24, 2024. Quote from Williams from *The Bloudy Tenent of Persecution for Cause of Conscience: and Mr. Cotton's Letter Examined and Answered* (London: J. Haddon, 1848), 435, https://archive.org/details/bloudytenentofpe00will_1/page/434/mode/2up.

103 **"The number, the industry, and the morality of the priesthood . . .":** James Madison, *Letter to Robert Walsh Jr., March 2, 1819,* letter From the National Archives, https://founders.archives.gov/documents/Madison/04-01-02-0378.

103 **"In France, I had almost always seen . . .":** Alexis de Tocqueville, *Democracy in America,* 2 vols., Phillips Bradley edition (New York: Alfred A. Knopf, 1945), 319–320.

104 **Andrew Seidel, constitutional lawyer:** Quotations from Andrew Seidel are taken from a personal conversation with Amanda Tyler on June 5, 2023.

106 **In the Virginia Chronicle in 1790:** John Leland, "The Virginia Chronicle," in *The Writings of the Late Elder John Leland* (New York: G.W. Wood,

1845), 107, 118. https://archive.org/details/writingsoflatee100lela/page/106/mode/2up.

106 *The Citizens of the United States:* George Washington, *Letter to the Hebrew Congregation in Newport, Rhode Island, August 18, 1790,* available on the website of the Touro Synagogue: https://tourosynagogue.org/history/george-washington-letter/washington-seixas-letters/.

109 *In states with an established and preferentially funded religion:* Dan Koev, "The Influence of State Favoritism on Established Religions and Their Competitors," *Politics and Religion* 16, no. 1 (2022): 1–31.

110 *Again, Baptist pastor John Leland wrote: The Writings of the Late Elder John Leland,* 278, https://archive.org/details/writingsoflatee100lela/page/278/mode/2up.

110 *"The church must be reminded . . .":* Martin Luther King Jr., *Strength to Love* (New York: Harper & Row, 1963), 59.

111 *"It is true, we are not disposed . . .":* Federal Farmer, "Letter IV, October 12, 1787," *The Complete Anti-Federalist, Vol. 2* (Chicago: University of Chicago Press, Herbert J. Storing, 1981), 249. Historians are uncertain of the exact identity of the "Federal Farmer," but many attribute the letters to Richard Henry Lee.

112 *Religious liberty is secured:* "The Bill of Rights: A Transcription," Article VI, accessed April 25, 2024, https://www.archives.gov/founding-docs/bill-of-rights-transcript.

112 *He writes, "The fundamental paradox of America's history . . .":* Michael I. Meyerson, *Endowed by Our Creator: The Birth of Religious Freedom in America* (New Haven, CT: Yale University Press, 2012), 10.

114 *Aziz explained that ensuring religious freedom:* Quotations from Sahar Aziz are taken from a personal conversation with Amanda Tyler on August 4, 2023.

115 *In the US Supreme Court's:* US Supreme Court decision in *McCreary County v. ACLU of Kentucky,* 545 U.S. 844 (2005), accessed April 25, 2024, https://supreme.justia.com/cases/federal/us/545/844/.

116 *"Nonetheless, the experience . . .":* Quotations from Rabbi David Saperstein are taken from a personal conversation with Amanda Tyler on August 8, 2023.

118 *Over the past decade:* For more on *Trinity Lutheran v. Comer, Espinoza v. Montana, Carson v. Makin,* and *Kennedy v. Bremerton,* see Amanda Tyler and Holly Hollman, "'Pro-Religion'? Conservative Supreme Court abandons Long-Standing Religious Liberty Principles," *USA Today,* October 5, 2022, https://www.usatoday.com/story/opinion/2022/10/05/supreme-court-ignores-precedents-protect-religious-liberty/8139768001/. For more on *The American Legion v. American Humanist Association,* see Amanda Tyler, "The Supreme Court Made the Bladensburg Cross a Special Case. Let's Keep It That Way," Religion

News Service, June 24, 2019, https://religionnews.com/2019/06/24
/the-supreme-court-made-a-special-case-of-the-bladensburg-cross-lets
-keep-it-that-way/.

118 *It is important to remember:* In the *Carson v. Makin* case, this principle is less clear. BJC, "BJC Blasts Supreme Court Decision in Carson v. Makin," press release, June 21, 2022, https://bjconline.org/bjc
-responds-to-carson-v-makin-decision/.

118 *Let's say that a Muslim citizen:* Dissent from Justice Elena Kagan in
Town of Grece v. Galloway, 572 U.S. 565 (2014), accessed April 25, 2024,
https://supreme.justia.com/cases/federal/us/572/565/.

STEP FIVE: TAKE ON CHRISTIAN NATIONALISM CLOSE TO HOME

126 *In her book* This America: The Case for the Nation: Jill Lepore, *This
America: The Case for the Nation* (New York: Liveright, 2019), 23.

127 *The difference between the two is stark:* Lepore, *This America*, 24.

129 *Should American flags be in church sanctuaries?:* J. Brent Walker,
"Should American Flags Be in Church Sanctuaries?" *Report from the
Capital* 66, no. 6 (June 2011): 4, https://bjconline.org/should-american
-flags-be-in-church-sanctuaries/.

132 *In June 2023, Faithful America:* Brian Kaylor and Beau Underwood,
"Preachers Confront Christian Nationalism," *Word&Way*, June 13, 2023,
https://wordandway.org/2023/06/13/preachers-confront-christian
-nationalism/.

133 *The point of Christ the King Sunday:* "Christ the King?" November
26, 2023, https://royallane.org/sermons/christ-the-king/.

135 *But if it's approached:* Quotations from Rev. Dr. Austin Carty are taken
from a personal conversation with Amanda Tyler on June 14, 2023.

139 *So, if you take one:* Pamela Cooper-White, "The Psychology of Christian Nationalism," event for the 11th annual Herbener Lecture, broadcast from King of Glory Lutheran Church in Dallas, Texas, November
16, 2023, 35:00, https://www.youtube.com/watch?v=f24lgir-es4.

139 *She said we should:* Cooper-White, "The Psychology of Christian
Nationalism," 37:38.

STEP SIX: ORGANIZE FOR CHANGE

145 *What do we mean by community:* Alexia Salvatierra and Peter Heltzel,
Faith-Rooted Organizing: Mobilizing the Church in Service to the World
(Downers Grove, IL: InterVarsity Press, 2013), 8.

146 *Faith-rooted organizing, according to Dr. Salvatierra and Dr. Heltzel:*
Salvatierra and Heltzel, *Faith-Rooted Organizing*, 9.

147 **Community organizing _is distinct:_** Salvatierra and Heltzel, _Faith-Rooted Organizing_, 8.

149 **_"I will state flatly that . . .":_** James Baldwin, "The Price May Be Too High," _New York Times,_ February 2, 1969, https://www.nytimes.com/1969/02/02/archives/the-price-may-be-too-high.html.

150 **_Dr. Salvatierra and Dr. Heltzel call these_ "kairos issues":** Salvatierra and Heltzel, _Faith-Rooted Organizing_, 66.

151 **_In the organizing model:_** Salvatierra and Heltzel, _Faith-Rooted Organizing_, 87.

153 **_"We recognize the natural impatience of people...":_** "White clergymen urge local Negros to withdraw from demonstrations," _The Birmingham News_, April 13, 1963, https://bplonline.contentdm.oclc.org/digital/collection/p4017coll2/id/746/.

154 **_I guess it is easy:_** Martin Luther King Jr., "Letter from Birmingham Jail," April 16, 1963, pages 6–7 of the copy digitized for The University of Alabama Libraries Special Collections, https://cdm17336.contentdm.oclc.org/digital/collection/p17336coll22/id/2663/rec/1.

STEP SEVEN: PROTECT RELIGIOUS FREEDOM IN PUBLIC SCHOOLS

159 **_"Talarico is something of a theological Clark Kent":_** Adam Wren, "He's Deeply Religious and a Democrat. He Might Be the Next Big Thing in Texas Politics," _Politico,_ June 16, 2023, https://www.politico.com/news/magazine/2023/06/16/james-talarico-texas-democrats-00101231.

160 **_I say this to you as a fellow Christian:_** https://twitter.com/jamestalarico/status/1653852600377196548?s=20, posted on Twitter (now called "X") on May 3, 2023, by @jamestalarico.

162 **_"And as a Christian myself . . .":_** Conversation between Amanda Tyler and James Talarico on May 6, 2023, available on YouTube at https://www.youtube.com/watch?v=N09gJWKpwiQ.

162 **_Research has shown that younger generations:_** "Support for Christian nationalist beliefs increases with age, with a significant break around age 50. Nearly four in ten Americans ages 65 and older (13% Adherents, 25% Sympathizers) and about one-third of Americans ages 50–64 (11% Adherents, 21% Sympathizers) support Christian nationalist beliefs, compared with only about one-quarter of those ages 30–49 and those ages 18–29." From Executive Summary of "Support for Christian Nationalism in All 50 States: Findings from PRRI's 2023 American Values Atlas," accessed April 17, 2014, https://www.prri.org/research/support-for-christian-nationalism-in-all-50-states/.

162 **_For several years, groups like the Congressional Prayer Caucus Foundation:_** "Report and Analysis on Religious Freedom Measures

Impacting Prayer and Faith in America, Congressional Prayer Caucus Foundation," available online via Religion Dispatches at https://religion dispatches.org/wp-content/uploads/2021/07/Religious-Freedom-Analysis -Report-2020-2021.pdf. Originally linked in article by Frederick Clarkson, "Exclusive: Christian Right Bill Mill, Project Blitz, Hasn't Gone Away, It's Just Gotten More Secretive," *Religion Dispatches* July 12, 2021, https://religiondispatches.org/exclusive-christian-right-bill-mill -project-blitz-hasnt-gone-away-its-just-gotten-more-secretive/.

163 *In the 2020–21 version of its legislative playbook:* "Report and Analysis on Religious Freedom Measures," 11.

163 *In August 2023, Louisiana became the seventeenth state:* Sarah Schwartz, "Louisiana's Public Schools Must Now Display 'In God We Trust' in Classrooms," *Education Week*, August 3, 2023, https://www.edweek.org /policy-politics/louisianas-public-schools-must-now-display-in-god-we -trust-in-classrooms/2023/08.

163 *The states passing these laws:* For example, "In God We Trust" laws passed in Arkansas in 2017, with 78 of 100 House members voting for it; in Tennessee in 2018, with 81 of 99 Tennessee House members voting for it; in and in Texas in 2021, with 106 of 145 House members voting for it.

164 *In a 6–3 decision, the Supreme Court:* Kennedy v. Bremerton School District, 142 S.Ct. 2407 (2022), accessed April 25, 2024, https://www.supreme court.gov/opinions/21pdf/21-418_i425.pdf.

164 *I say that the* **Kennedy** *decision:* Kennedy v. Bremerton, 142 S.Ct. 2407, 2418 (2022).

165 *As I lamented at the time:* Amanda Tyler (@AmandaTylerBJC), "3/5 Instead, the Court focused solely on the religious exercise," Twitter, June 27, 2022, 10:42 a.m., https://twitter.com/AmandaTylerBJC /status/1541446977883348992.

168 *He published a study with:* Mark Chancey, "Reading, Writing and Religion II: Texas Public School Bible Courses in 2011–2012," Texas Freedom Network Education Fund, https://www.smu.edu/~/media /Images/News/PDFs/Mark-Chancey-Reading-Writing-Religion-study .ashx?la=en&la=en.

169 *"Schools are our society's primary institution . . .":* Quotations from Dr. Mark Chancey are taken from a personal conversation with Amanda Tyler on June 15, 2023.

171 *There are 613 in the Hebrew Bible:* Conversation between Amanda Tyler and James Talarico on May 6, 2023.

176 *Christian programs in those states:* "State-By-State Laws," accessed April 25, 2024, https://releasedtime.org/statelaws.

177 *For many Muslims:* Quotations from Sahar Aziz are taken from a personal conversation with Amanda Tyler on August 4, 2023.

178 *In 2022, in Dearborn, Michigan:* Tom Perkins, "Conservative Muslims Join Forces with Christian Right on Michigan Book Bans," *Guardian*, October 16, 2022, https://www.theguardian.com/us-news/2022/oct/16/dearborn-michigan-book-bans.

182 *A group of professional chaplains:* "Texas Chaplains Say No to Public School Chaplains," September 12, 2023, https://bjconline.org/wp-content/uploads/2023/09/UPDATED-LETTER_-Texas-Chaplains-Say-No-to-Public-School-Chaplain-Programs.pdf. First version of the letter was released on August 22, 2023, and the updated release has additional signatories. Original letter here: https://bjconline.org/wp-content/uploads/2023/08/LETTER_-Texas-Chaplains-Say-No-to-Public-School-Chaplain-Programs.pdf.

183 *She described the proposed poster:* Britt Luby, "'Thou Shalt Not Covet Thy Neighbor's Wife' and Other Posters I Do Not Want in a First Grade Classroom," Baptist News Global, April 21, 2023, https://baptistnews.com/article/thou-shalt-not-covet-thy-neighbors-wife-and-other-posters-i-do-not-want-in-a-first-grade-classroom/.

STEP EIGHT: TAKE YOUR PLACE IN THE PUBLIC SQUARE

188 *Christian nationalism is a form:* Conversation took place during "Faith Under Fire: An Examination of Global Religious Persecution," October 25, 2023, https://oversight.house.gov/hearing/faith-under-fire-an-examination-of-global-religious-persecution/.

189 *He raised up each of you:* House Session, Part 1, U.S. House of Representatives, October 25, 2023, C-SPAN, accessed April 24, 2024, https://www.c-span.org/video/?531374-1/house-session-part-1.

192 *The US Citizenship and Immigration Services tells:* "Should I Consider U.S. Citizenship?" US Citizenship and Immigration Service, accessed April 8, 2024, https://www.uscis.gov/citizenship/learn-about-citizenship/should-i-consider-us-citizenship.

194 *In a speech for BJC's National Religious Liberty Conference:* "Barbara Jordan's 1986 Speech on Church-State Separation Resonates Today," *Respecting Religion* podcast, November 30, 2023, https://bjconline.org/s5-ep-07-barbara-jordans-1986-speech-on-church-state-separation-resonates-today/. Original speech given in October 1986 and archived on cassette tape at BJC headquarters.

194 *In my opinion, the church is forbidden:* "Barbara Jordan's 1986 Speech on Church-State."

196 *In the same* **New Yorker** *story:* Eliza Griswold, "A Pennsylvania Lawmaker and the Resurgence of Christian Nationalism," *New Yorker*, May 9, 2021, https://www.newyorker.com/news/on-religion/a-pennsylvania-lawmaker-and-the-resurgence-of-christian-nationalism.

196 *Some politicians continue to proudly claim:* Rep. Marjorie Taylor Greene interview with Tayler Hansen of Next News Network, posted on Twitter July 24, 2022: https://twitter.com/NextNewsNetwork /status/1551204108471861248.

196 *One of the most prominent Christian:* Tara Isabella Burton, "Trump-Allied Pastor Tells Worshippers 'America Is a Christian Nation,'" *Vox,* June 25, 2018, https://www.vox.com/2018/6/25/17502170/pastor-robert -jeffress-america-christian-nation-trump-dallas-baptist.

198 *I rise today to bring attention:* US Representative Jared W. Huffman (@RepHuffman), "It's clear from @BJContheHill & @FFRF's report," Twitter, March 31, 2022, 5:43 p.m., https://twitter.com/RepHuffman/status /1509662789719187457.

199 *"It's easy for an outsider...":* Quotations from Rep. Jared Huffman are taken from a personal conversation with Amanda Tyler on August 4, 2023.

201 *In 1954, a three-phrase change was added:* Internal Revenue Code 501(c)(3), accessed April 8, 2024, https://www.irs.gov/charities-non -profits/charitable-organizations/exempt-purposes-internal-revenue -code-section-501c3.

201 *The Johnson Amendment:* "Charities, Churches and Politics," Internal Revenue Service, accessed April 8, 2024, https://www.irs.gov/newsroom /charities-churches-and-politics.

202 *Then in February 2017:* Amanda Tyler, "Politicize Our Charities and Churches? No, Thanks," Religion News Service, February 9, 2017, https://religionnews.com/2017/02/09/politicize-our-charities -and-churches-no-thanks.

202 *Plus, the Johnson Amendment protects:* For more on how removing the Johnson Amendment is unnecessary, unwise, and unwanted, see "Supporting the Johnson Amendment," BJC resource, accessed April 25, 2024, https://bjconline.org/wp-content/uploads/2019/06/Supporting -the-Johnson-Amendment-2019.pdf.

202 *A diverse array of secular:* "Community Letter in Support of Nonpartisanship," September 5, 2017, https://www.councilofnonprofits.org /files/media/documents/2022/community-letter-in-support-of -nonpartisanship-5-12-update.pdf; "Faith Voices" letter from religious leaders, August 16, 2017, https://static1.squarespace.com /static/590789143e00be8692d38a5c/t/59935d54be42d66fd5660285 /1502829911755/FinalLetter_SENATE_header. PDF; and a letter from faith groups opposing a change in the tax law, November 13, 2017, https://bjconline.org/wp-content/uploads/2017/11/11.13.17-Faith -Organization-Letter-Opposing-Politicization-of-Houses-of-Worship .pdf.

202 *Since that first announcement:* Jack Jenkins, "Johnson Amendment Remains Intact in Latest Omnibus Spending Bill," Religion News

Service, March 22, 2018, https://religionnews.com/2018/03/22/johnson
-amendment-remains-intact-in-latest-omnibus-spending-bill/.

204 *"The church was the heart and soul . . ."*: US Representative John Lewis
(D-Georgia) Testimony on the Houses of Worship Political Speech Protection Act, Congressional Record Volume 148, Number 126, October
1, 2002, https://www.govinfo.gov/content/pkg/CREC-2002-10-01/html
/CREC-2002-10-01-pt1-PgH6912.htm.

204 *In October 1960:* Steven Levingston, "John F. Kennedy, Martin Luther King
Jr., and the Phone Call That Changed History," *Time*, June 20, 2017, https://
time.com/4817240/martin-luther-king-john-kennedy-phone-call/.

205 *"[T]he role that is mine . . ."*: Rev. Dr. Martin Luther King Jr., "Statement
on Presidential Endorsement," press release of the Southern Christian Leadership Conference, November 1, 1960, https://kinginstitute
.stanford.edu/king-papers/documents/statement-presidential-endorsement.

205 *"I never intend to be a religious bigot. . . ."*: Freedom Crusade Com-
mittee, Pamphlet, "The Case of Martin Luther King," October 27–
November 7, 1960, available in *The Papers of Martin Luther King, Jr.*
(Berkeley: University of California Press, 2005), 539.

206 *In 1857, Frederick Douglass said:* Frederick Douglass, "West India
Emancipation," Two Speeches by Frederick Douglass (Rochester, NY:
C.P. Dewey, 1857), 22, https://www.loc.gov/resource/mss11879.21039
/?sp=22&st=image&r=-0.737,0.024,2.474,1.49,0.